D1388162

90 Days in

Ruth, Jeremiah & 1 Corinthians

thegoodbook
COMPANY

EXPLORE BY THE BOOK
Ruth, Jeremiah & 1 Corinthians

© The Good Book Company, 2016

Published by:
The Good Book Company

Tel (US): 866 244 2165
Tel (UK): 0333 123 0880
Email (US): info@thegoodbook.com
Email (UK): info@thegoodbook.co.uk

Websites:

North America: www.thegoodbook.com
UK: www.thegoodbook.co.uk
Australia: www.thegoodbook.com.au
New Zealand: www.thegoodbook.co.nz

Unless indicated, all Scripture references are taken from the HOLY BIBLE, NEW INTERNATIONAL VERSION. Copyright © 2011 Biblica, Inc.™ Used by permission.

ISBN: 9781784981235

Printed in Denmark by Nørhaven

Design by André Parker

EXPLORE
BY THE BOOK

90 DAYS IN

Ruth, Jeremiah & 1 Corinthians

with

Mark Dever
& Mike McKinley

Contents

Introduction

"The words of the LORD are flawless, like silver
purified in a crucible, like gold refined seven times."
(Psalm 12 v 6)

This book is not an end in itself. It is a means of accessing the treasures of a far greater book. Its words are valuable only to the extent that they help you to enjoy the infinite value of words that are perfectly true, gloriously beautiful, and utterly wonderful—the words of the LORD.

It is a magnificent thing, in a world which is used to mistakes, to deceit, and to confusion, to be able to read flawless, pure, refined words. And that is what you do each time you open your Bible. God does not make errors in anything he says. He does not obscure the truth, by accident or by design. He does not fail to do anything he has said he will do.

That is why this devotional is an "open Bible devotional"—that is, you will need to keep your Bible open, on your lap or on your screen, as you use these studies. You'll be asked questions that bring you to examine and think hard about the text. The aim of the authors is to cause you to spend more time thinking about God's words than their words.

So, rather than seeing these devotionals as snacks, view them as meals. Set aside half an hour in your day to work through the study, and to respond to what you have seen. They are best done daily—but the most crucial thing is for you to find a pattern that is sustainable—better five studies a week for life, than seven studies a week for only a week!

Further, since every word of the Lord is flawless, we need to read every word in the Scriptures, rather than sticking to our favorite passages, or to an author's favorites. So *Explore by the Book* works, verse by verse, through whole books or large sections of the Bible. You will be moving through both famous books and not-so-popular ones, and within each book through much-used passages and less traveled parts. Expect to discover new favorite passages and memory verses that you had never read or noticed or appreciated before!

At the same time, God's word is not always easy to understand. Whether we are completely new to reading it, or have mined its riches many times, all of us still experience "huh?" moments as we struggle to grasp its meaning! So in this devotional series, some of the greatest Bible teachers in the evangelical world help you to dig up the Bible's treasures, and explain their more opaque aspects. They will show you how what you are reading fits into the great overall story of the Scriptures, and prompt you to apply what you have read to your life.

God's word is not simply pure—it is also purifying. It is the way his Spirit works in his people to challenge and change us. It is designed to move us to worship him with our lips, in our hearts, and through our lives. Each day, you will see one (or both) of these headings: *Apply*, and *Pray*. Use these sections to turn what you have read in God's word into words to speak back to God, and into ways you will change your life in response to God.

At the end of each study you'll find a journaling page, for you to record your response to what you have read, either in words or in drawings. Use these pages as you are led to—we all have different ways of making sure we remember what we have seen in the Scriptures, and of responding to those Scriptures. But here are a couple of very straightforward suggestions that you might like to try:

Before you work through the study, read the passage and record...

The Highlight: the truth about God that has most struck you.

The Query: the questions you have about what you have read (and your best attempt at answering them)

The Change: the major way you feel the Spirit is prompting you to change either your attitudes, or your actions, as a result of what you have read.

After you have done the study, record:

One sentence summing up how God has spoken to you through his word.

A short prayer in response to what you have seen.

I hope you enjoy these 90 days listening to the flawless words of the LORD. Be sure that they will excite, change, challenge and comfort you. Be praying that God would be using his word to bless you. There is literally nothing like the words of the LORD.

Carl Laferton, Editorial Director
The Good Book Company

Note: This devotional is based on the NIV2011 Bible translation, but it will also work well with either ESV or NIV1984 translations.

Meet the Authors

MARK DEVER is Senior Pastor at Capitol Hill Baptist Church in Washington, D.C., and President of 9Marks Ministries. Married to Connie with two adult children, he is the author of many books including *Nine Marks of a Healthy Church* and *The Compelling Community*. He has an M.Div. from Gordon-Conwell, a Th.M from The Southern Baptist Theological Seminary, and a Ph.D. from Cambridge, UK.

MIKE McKINLEY is Senior Pastor of Sterling Park Baptist Church, Virginia. Before that, he served on the pastoral staff of Capitol Hill Baptist Church under Mark Dever. Married to Karen with five children, he is the author of books that include *Passion*, *Church Planting in Hard Places* and *Did the Devil Make me do it?* Mike received his M.Div. from Westminster Theological Seminary.

A Family Disaster

Ruth 1 v 1-5

Ruth opens in "the days when the judges ruled," and, it seems from the end of the book, that the events described here took place around 1100 BC.

The period of the judges was marked by the lack of a king and general disobedience to the law of the LORD (Judges 21 v 25), but Ruth's story is going to show us how God used the courage of two women to give Israel the king that they needed.

The Family Tree

Read Ruth 1 v 1-5

The story of this family is complicated.

Can you sketch out a "family tree" (in your head or on paper) establishing these people's relationships to each other?

- *Elimelek (meaning "God is king")*
- *Naomi*
- *Mahlon (meaning "sickly")*
- *Kilion (meaning "wasting")*
- *Orpah*
- *Ruth (4 v 10 gives more information)*

The Story

The book of Ruth begins as the story of one woman's personal tragedy.

What was the problem that set these events in motion (1 v 1)? What did Elimelek do in response?

What happened to Elimelek (v 3)?

What did the sons do (v 4)? What happened to them (v 5)?

How much time goes by in the first five verses (v 4)?

What did Naomi have at the beginning of the passage?

What does she have at the end?

One of the key challenges early in Ruth is figuring out how we are supposed to feel about the characters and their actions.

God had warned that he would send Israel famine if they worshiped idols (Deuteronomy 32 v 23-44). So it's possible—given the state of Israel during the time of the judges (see Judges 2 v 10-19; 21 v 25)—that Israel is experiencing God's discipline.

Further, it's probable that Elimelek was wrong to flee to Moab (a foreign nation), away from the promised land. It may be significant that at first Elimelek went to "sojourn" (Ruth 1 v 1, ESV) in Moab, then they "remained there" (v 2, ESV), and finally they "lived there" (v 4, ESV).

The people of Israel had a long and unpleasant history with the people of Moab, and God had told Israel that marrying foreign women was dangerous for their faith (Deuteronomy 7 v 1-4; see 1 Kings 11 v 1-6). Elimelek's sons marrying Moabite women would have sounded like bad news to the first readers of Ruth.

⊙ Apply

Where in your life are there ways in which what seems most sensible, and what would be obedient to God are at odds with each other? What would risky obedience look like in those areas?

~ Notes and Prayers ~

_____

_____

_____

_____

_____

_____

_____

_____

_____

_____

_____

_____

_____

_____

_____

_____

_____

_____

_____

_____

_____

_____

Day

2

Where You Go, I Go

Ruth 1 v 6-18

Naomi finds herself alone in a foreign land with two foreign daughters-in-law. What will she (and they) do next?

Naomi's Decision

Read Ruth 1 v 6-9

An unmarried or widowed woman in that society was very vulnerable, especially economically. Ruth and Orpah were young enough to pursue another marriage, but Naomi would have had very few ways to provide for herself.

Why did Naomi choose to return to Judah (v 6)?

What can we tell from these verses about Naomi's relationship with her daughters-in-law? Why do you think that Naomi wanted them to return to their homes?

The Response

Read Ruth 1 v 10-15

Ruth and Orpah respond to Naomi with protests (v 10), and you can understand why. They were family; they had been together for ten years and endured terrible losses in each other's company. But still, Naomi insists that they return (v 11). The expectation in the Israelite law was that the brother of the deceased would marry his widow in order to make sure that she was provided for, but this was not going to happen here.

How does Naomi seek to convince them that she cannot provide for them (v 12-13)?

What does Orpah do in response (v 14-15)?

Ruth's God

Read Ruth 1 v 16-18

There are several signals in these verses that through her relationship with Naomi, Ruth had come to a place where she wanted to be a follower of the true God:

- In verse 17, she refers to him by his personal name (the Lord—"Yahweh").

- The land of Israel belonged to Yahweh in a special way. Ruth wanted to live there (v 16).

- The people of Israel were Yahweh's people. Ruth wanted to be part of them (v 16).

- In ancient times, people wanted to be buried in the land of their gods (so that they could be protected in the afterlife). Ruth wants to be buried in the place where Yahweh is worshiped (v 17).

Ruth's reaction is very striking in two ways. First, her suffering has not embittered her towards the Lord. Suffering makes us either run to God, or away from him. Ruth chose the first. Second, despite not being an Israelite, Ruth was confident that God would accept her. The rest of the book will show whether or not she is right.

⊙ Apply

Do you ever have an Orpah moment, banking on worldly security instead of risking all to live as a follower of God? What would change if you lived with Ruth-like faith?

~ Notes and Prayers ~

Call Me Bitter

Ruth 1 v 19-22

So far, we have not seen much of how Naomi feels about her suffering. Her return to her hometown will give her an opportunity to reflect on what has happened.

The Return

Read Ruth 1 v 19-21

The people of Bethlehem probably did not know what had become of Naomi and Elimelek and their sons during their decade in a foreign land. So when she appeared in town without her family (but with Ruth instead!), it created quite a commotion.

When the women of Bethlehem ask if this could be Naomi, she takes the opportunity to express her feelings about what has happened to her. She asks not to be called "Naomi" (meaning "pleasant"), but rather, "Mara" (meaning "bitter").

Why does Naomi think that Mara would be a more fitting name for her?

How was she "full" when she left (v 21)? How is she "empty" now?

Naomi's Theology

Naomi's suffering reveals what she believes about God. She believes that the LORD is responsible for her pain; the Almighty has "brought misfortune" upon her (v 21).

She seems to believe that her suffering is evidence that the LORD is displeased with her in some way; he has "afflicted" her.

Read Psalm 135 v 6-7; Daniel 4 v 34-35; Isaiah 45 v 7

What do these passages tell us about God's involvement in what happens to us, including painful events?

Can you think of times in the Bible when God used someone's suffering to bring about a greater good? (Hint: Try Genesis 45 v 4-11; Acts 16 v 25-34.)

Good Things to Come

Read Ruth 1 v 22

If this is your first time reading the book of Ruth, then verse 22 might seem unimportant—just the author setting the scene for his readers. But if you know what is about to happen, then you know that the timing of events (at the beginning of the barley harvest) is evidence that God is at work to bless Naomi.

⊙ Apply

Can you trust the Lord's good plan even when it involves you suffering or losing out?

Naomi will discover through the events of the next three chapters how God is using her suffering for her good, the good of others, and the fulfillment of his plans. Living this side of the worst moment of human suffering in history—the cross—we can already be confident that this is how God uses all the events in our lives.

How do you particularly need to hear this, either as a comfort or challenge, today?

~ Notes and Prayers ~

_____

_____

_____

_____

_____

_____

_____

_____

_____

_____

_____

_____

_____

_____

_____

_____

_____

_____

_____

_____

_____

Day

4

A Short-term Solution

Ruth 2 v 1-13

Naomi's lack of a husband and sons was not only sad; it was a financial crisis. There were no grocery stores; how would she find food without land or crops of her own?

Read Ruth 2 v 1-13

Introducing Boaz

Ruth's plan (v 2) was to find a field and glean grain there. Landowners in those days would leave the edges of the fields unharvested and leave behind any grain that fell to the ground as it was being bundled by workers. The poor and needy could then come and "glean" this extra grain and have something to eat.

It is at this point that we are introduced to Boaz, the other main character in our story. In just a few short verses, we learn some very important information about him:

• He is a member of Elimelek's family, related to Naomi through marriage.

• He is a "man of standing" (v 1).

• He is a wealthy and influential man, a landowner and an employer.

In the Field

When Boaz finds out who Ruth is, he instructs her to continue gleaning in his fields. As you can imagine, an unmarried foreign woman like Ruth was very vulnerable while she was at work in the fields. But Boaz had instructed his workers not to touch her; in fact she was even welcome to the water they had drawn for themselves.

How do you think Ruth felt when she first walked into a stranger's field in a foreign land and began to collect grain for herself?

What fears might she have had?

How does she respond to Boaz's kindness (v 10 and 13)?

It is clear that Boaz is a faithful, law-keeping Israelite. Look at the LORD's commands and see how the author of Ruth is showing the reader Boaz's character: *read Deuteronomy 10 v 19; 24 v 19; Leviticus 19 v 9-10.*

⊙ Apply

Boaz understands that his provision for Ruth is actually the LORD's kindness to her (Ruth 2 v 11-12). The LORD's love is often communicated to us through the love and kindness of his people.

How can you help one of God's children experience his love today?

This was the time of the Judges, when "everyone did what was right in his own eyes" (Judges 21 v 25, ESV). But Boaz did not—he did what was right in God's eyes. Life in his field was different, and better, because God's law ruled there.

How can you, and your church, provide a distinctive way of living to those around you— one that is godlier, more welcoming, and safer?

~ Notes and Prayers ~

Day

5

Filled to Overflowing

Ruth 2 v 14-23

Now, after so much pain and such a lot of uncertainty and struggle, Ruth and Naomi begin to see the hand of the LORD at work, through Boaz.

Plenty to Eat

Read Ruth 2 v 14-18

Boaz shows great kindness to Ruth, feeding her as if she were part of his work crew. He gives her free access to his fields and a safe place to work (v 22), and he even tells his workers to drop extra grain for her to gather. At the end of the day, Ruth has gathered and prepared more barley than she is likely able to carry. This situation carries on throughout the harvest. The main threat to Ruth and Naomi has been taken care of—they will have enough food to survive.

God provided for Ruth abundantly, but she also had to work diligently in the fields.

What does this tell us about the relationship between God's promise to care for us and our responsibility to work to provide for ourselves? In what ways might we get this relationship wrong?

Elimelek led his family out of Bethlehem—and out of God's land—because of a famine in the land (1 v 1).

How should we think about the times when God chooses not to provide for us abundantly?

⊘ Pray

Take time to thank God for providing all of the things that you truly need. Thank him for what he has not provided, and ask him to help you to see what you "lack" as an opportunity to grow in godly contentment and gratitude. *Read 1 Timothy 6 v 6-10.*

The Pieces Come Together

Read Ruth 2 v 19-23

Naomi is excited to see Ruth come home with food, but she seems even more excited when she realizes that the man who has shown Ruth kindness is none other than Boaz, her husband's relative! He is a "close relative" and a "guardian-redeemer" (what that means is about to become very important!).

Ruth and Naomi had returned from Moab empty-handed (1 v 21), but now both have plenty of food. The LORD is no longer described as the Almighty who has dealt bitterly with Naomi, but he is called the one who "has not stopped showing his kindness" (2 v 20).

Do you think Naomi wished she could take back what she had said in 1 v 20-21?

⊘ Apply

Do you ever find that your heart is fickle, complaining about God's provision for you one moment and then joyful when you later get what you want? What would be a godlier attitude in these times?

~ Notes and Prayers ~

Day
6

Beyond the Harvest

Ruth 3 v 1-9

The LORD had provided for Ruth and Naomi's needs, but it still wasn't clear what would happen to them once the barley harvest was over.

A Bold Plan

Read Ruth 3 v 1-9

In order to understand this story, we need to understand the concept of a "guardian-redeemer." Naomi has already called Boaz a "guardian-redeemer" (2 v 20), and in this passage we see it referred to in 3 v 9 (and later in v 12-13 too). In this context, redemption involved a widow marrying her husband's next closest relative in order to keep property in the family and provide an heir for the deceased (see Leviticus 25 v 23-25 and Deuteronomy 25 v 5-6). Naomi knows that Boaz (as a close relative of Ruth's deceased husband Mahlon) could marry Ruth and provide for her.

But will he?

A Long-term Strategy

Re-read Ruth 3 v 1-5

What does Naomi want for Ruth?

What does she want Ruth to do?

It's not clear what is meant by Naomi's instruction to uncover Boaz's feet. It may be an ancient custom that we don't understand, or it may just be a way to wake someone up gently.

The Plan Unfolds

Re-read Ruth 3 v 6-9

How did Ruth do what Naomi said?

In what ways did she go off the script?

Boaz is understandably surprised to find Ruth at his feet (v 8), but Ruth doesn't hesitate to ask him to spread the corner of his garment over her (referring to a custom by which a man would propose marriage). This plan involved quite a risk for Ruth; Boaz had been kind and generous to her, but there was no way to know how he would respond to her.

⊙ Apply

Ruth provides an example of what godly womanhood looks like. In fact, in the Hebrew Bible, the book of Ruth followed directly after the book of Proverbs. As you were reading, you would go from the famous description of a godly woman in Proverbs 31 v 10-31 directly into the story of Ruth.

Think back over the story up to this point. In what ways has Ruth demonstrated strength, bravery and godliness?

What does the world around us say matters most in a woman? How is Ruth's character and conduct similar and/or different?

What do you prize in yourself, or in your spouse or daughters or sisters in your church family? Is it what Ruth showcases, or what the world exalts?

Does anything need to change? How would prioritizing Ruth-like qualities be positive for you, or for the women around you?

~ Notes and Prayers ~

Day

7

The Suspense Builds

Ruth 3 v 10-18

Naomi's plan seems to be working out perfectly, but there is a significant obstacle.

Boaz's Response

Read Ruth 3 v 10-11

Ruth had suggested that Boaz marry her and act as her "redeemer."

Why might he not want to marry someone like Ruth? Why does he say that he does in fact want to marry her?

Why does he think that Ruth might not want to marry him?

Some suggest that there is something inappropriate going on in Ruth's late-night approach to Boaz; but his response in verse 11 (calling Ruth a "woman of noble character") makes it clear that this wasn't the case. In fact, in verse 14 Boaz seems concerned that Ruth should leave before sunrise so that her reputation would not be unfairly sullied.

The Obstacle

Read Ruth 3 v 12-18

In the system of ancient Israel, the right to act as a redeemer went to the closest relative of a deceased person. Boaz reveals that there is someone who must be offered the opportunity before he can act. By now, we have come to root for Boaz and Ruth; they seem to make a great couple! And so the news that there is another redeemer seems like a problem. But there's good news buried in there; one way or the other, someone is going to act as a redeemer for Ruth and Naomi.

What does Boaz do for Ruth before she leaves? What explanation does he give for his actions?

How does Naomi advise Ruth in verse 18?

⊙ Apply

Boaz insisted that Ruth must not return to Naomi empty-handed. When she returned with the promise of a husband and a cloak full of food, things had come full circle for Naomi. In 1 v 9, she had asked the LORD to provide rest and a husband for her daughter-in-law; now it's clear that the LORD has heard her cry.

How does that encourage you to take your concerns and problems to the Lord? (Read Philippians 4 v 6 and 1 Peter 5 v 6-7.)

⊙ Pray

Think through the things that tempt you to be anxious as you think about the future. Take them to the Lord in prayer and ask for his help.

~ Notes and Prayers ~

_____

_____

_____

_____

_____

_____

_____

_____

_____

_____

_____

_____

_____

_____

_____

_____

_____

_____

_____

_____

_____

_____

_____

_____

_____

___Day___
___8___

The Redeemer Question

Ruth 4 v 1-12

B oaz wants to marry Ruth—but according to ancient custom, another man has the right to claim her first. This is not a done deal yet.

Too Good to Pass Up

Read Ruth 4 v 1-4

The morning after Ruth's daring late-night proposal, Boaz springs into action. In the presence of the city elders, he explains the opportunity: Naomi is selling the parcel of land that belonged to Elimelek.

What important detail is Boaz leaving out?

How does the redeemer respond to this opportunity for a lucrative real-estate investment?

This doesn't seem right. We have been led to think that Boaz and Ruth will be together; the story can't end this way!

The author does a masterful job of building suspense. Look how he uses the words "just as" (v 1) to impress on us how extraordinary it is that things worked out in just the way that they did. We have seen the same thing back in 2 v 3-4, where Ruth happens to wander into a field and "just then" Elimelek's relative Boaz came along.

What do these "coincidences" show us about the way that God is involved in the details of our lives?

⊙ Apply

How does God's involvement help you:

• *be patient in times of trouble?*

• *be thankful in times of prosperity?*

• *be confident as you look to the future?*

Oh, did I Mention...?

Read Ruth 4 v 5-10

In verse 5, Boaz reveals that there's more to the deal. Anyone who wants to redeem Elimelek's land will have to marry the widow of his son as well. The redeemer doesn't want to make that kind of financial commitment, so he passes his right of redemption on to Boaz.

How do they formalize the deal (v 7-8)?

What is the result of this transaction, according to Boaz (v 9-10)?

How are Boaz's priorities different from those of the unnamed redeemer?

A Blessing

Read Ruth 4 v 11-12

The people at the gates wish Ruth and Boaz well. There's irony here, for the stories of the women they mention—Rachel and Leah, and Tamar—were not always easy or smooth. But the LORD had used each of those women to build up the family of Israel and to further God's plans to bless his people.

⊙ Pray

We can't ask for more than to be used by God to build up his people and further his plans. Pray this for yourself now, and then pray it for some others in your church who you are close to.

~ Notes and Prayers ~

Day

9

A Happy Ending

Ruth 4 v 13-22

As the story comes to a happy conclusion, the author "zooms out" and shows us the bigger picture of what God has really been doing through Ruth's life.

There is a Redeemer

Read Ruth 4 v 13-17

Boaz acts as Ruth's redeemer in this story.

But who is Naomi's redeemer (v 14)? What will he do for her (v 15)?

Obed is Ruth's child. Why do you think they say that a son has been born to Naomi (v 17)?

Who is Naomi's great-great grandson (v 17)?

It's significant that the women praise the LORD for not leaving Naomi without a redeemer, for in the Old Testament the LORD himself is said to be the Redeemer of his people (Psalm 19 v 14). In the New Testament, Jesus is the one who brings this redemption (see Galatians 3 v 13-14).

How is the redemption in the book of Ruth a picture of what Jesus did for us through his death and resurrection?

A Strange Ending

Read Ruth 4 v 18-22

The book of Ruth tells a compelling story, but a list of names seems like an anti-climactic ending!

How many of the names in this genealogy do you recognize?

For the author of Ruth, King David would have been the high point of God's plan to bless his people. To be in his family line was a thrilling privilege. Sitting where we do in history, we know a greater One was promised to that family (2 Samuel 7 v 12-16)—and we know who he is (Matthew 1 v 1-17)!

Though Israel sometimes forgot it, God's plan was never merely to bless their nation but the entire world through them (Genesis 12 v 1-3). Here, God hard-wires that truth into Israel's story by giving their greatest king a foreign great-grandmother. The nations were included among David's ancestors!

The book opened with a reminder of the days of the judges, when no king ruled in Israel. The ending shows us that even when things were dark, God was at work to bring a faithful king to his people. From our perspective, we can see that in the bigger picture, God was using Ruth to bring about the still greater King Jesus!

⊙ Apply

It is very unlikely that Ruth lived to see her great-grandson become king. In many ways, the great point of her life was not realized until well after she was dead.

How does that encourage you to be faithful in the ordinary details of your life and trust the Lord with the results?

⊙ Pray

Thank the Lord for sending Ruth's descendant to redeem you from your sins.

~ Notes and Prayers ~

Problems, Problems

1 Corinthians 1 v 1-3

The church Paul had established in Corinth was young, full of life, and just as full of problems. As Paul sat down to write to them, they were threatened with self-destruction.

How should Paul start? Which of the deadly issues would he tackle first? None...

Read 1 Corinthians 1 v 1-3

A Church that is Owned

Who does the church in Corinth belong to (v 2)?

Which means that God cares about their church—and yours and mine, too.

What word does Paul next use to describe them (v 2)?

This word means "declared holy and righteous."

Where is this made available (v 2)?

Christians, whatever their weaknesses, mistakes and challenges, don't need to labor under condemnation. Through faith in God's Son, Jesus' holiness and righteousness are given to us. If we are Christians, we are sanctified. Not through the goodness of our efforts, but through the object of our faith—the Lord Jesus.

⊙ Apply

God sees you as "sanctified in Christ Jesus." How should this affect the way you see yourself?

A Church that is Called

What are the Corinthian Christians "called to be" (v 2)?

They need to become set apart, pure, godly, in how they think and speak and live. But aren't they already sanctified?! Are Christians set apart, or not?!

God has declared Christians holy through faith in Christ. Our status is "holy." But God also calls Christians to become holy, to have lives which more fully reflect Jesus Christ. We're to live more and more as the people God has made us to be.

⊙ Apply

In what three areas do you most struggle to live in a holy way?

How will knowing you are already sanctified motivate you to live in a more holy way; and then comfort you when you fail to?

A Church that Enjoys

What two things does Paul say the Corinthian Christians enjoy (v 3)?

As we'll see, neither undeserved mercy nor friendship and calm were hallmarks of this congregation!

So why do you think Paul begins by reminding them that these are the product of their relationship with God, through Christ?

With all the problems evident in Corinth, we might expect Paul to skip his opening encouragements. But the reason he doesn't is because of all the problems there. When we face difficulties as Christians, we need most of all to remember we are Christians: sanctified, called to be holy, enjoying grace and peace.

⊗ Pray

Re-read 1 Corinthians 1 v 1-3. Thank God that these things are true of you right now!

~ Notes and Prayers ~

_____

_____

_____

_____

_____

_____

_____

_____

_____

_____

_____

_____

_____

_____

_____

_____

_____

_____

_____

_____

_____

_____

_____

_____

_____

Day

II

Count your Blessings

1 Corinthians 1 v 4-9

Paul will need to correct and challenge this church in many areas. But first he wants them to count their blessings. And what blessings they have as those who "call on the name of our Lord Jesus Christ" (v 2)!

The Blessing of Grace

Read 1 Corinthians 1 v 4

The church in Corinth had been founded by Paul. Since then, it had been full of problems. And, as we'll see, there was some dissent toward Paul himself.

What is astonishing about what Paul is doing here?

Whatever challenges this church faces, or poses, the most important thing about its members is that they have received God's grace. Which is cause for great thanks!

⊘ Pray

Every true Christian, however much they are struggling, should prompt us to give thanks. Each congregation of Christians, however problematic, is a triumph of God's grace.

Pause now to praise God for Christians you know. Praise him particularly for any Christians who have caused you problems or heartache.

The Blessing of Knowledge

Read 1 Corinthians 1 v 5-6

Corinth was a place that valued knowledge. Paul reminds these Christians that in Christ they have the richest knowledge possible. In Christ they have found the purpose of their lives, the way they can be forgiven, the way they can know God himself. What better knowledge is there?

Where does Paul say his claims about Christ are shown to be true (v 6)?

⊘ Apply

How is your life a display of the truth of the gospel? Are there any ways you could display it more clearly?

The Blessing of Certainty

Read 1 Corinthians 1 v 7-8

What can Christians look forward to (v 7-8)?

How can struggling Christians be certain they will reach this future (v 8a)?

Our eternal well-being rests in hands safer and more powerful than our own!

The Blessing of Fellowship

Read 1 Corinthians 1 v 9

What has God called us into?

The Christian life is not about rituals, or rules: it's about relationship. God has given us the best he has—his Son.

⊘ Apply

Grace. Knowledge. Certainty. Fellowship. All these are yours as a Christian.

How do these things make you feel? How do they remind you to focus on, and pray about, what you have been given, rather than on what you haven't?

~ Notes and Prayers ~

○
Day
12

Multiplying Divisions

1 Corinthians 1 v 10-31

Division causes conflict, suffering and sadness. Division in the church is even more tragic, since it goes against Christ's desire that his people enjoy "complete unity" (John 17 v 23). So how can a church stay united?

Know Christ

Read 1 Corinthians 1 v 10-16

What do the Christians seem to have been arguing about (v 11-12)?

What point do you think Paul is making in verse 13?

Corinthian culture exalted particular orators, and argued over which was best—not so different from celebrity culture today. This promotion of one personality over another had permeated the church, and it was obscuring the uniqueness of Christ, the only Person who had been "crucified for you" (v 13).

How does, or would, this mistake look in your church today?

Accept Foolishness

Read 1 Corinthians 1 v 17-25

What is the gospel message about (v 17-18)?

What are the two responses to this message (v 18)?

What the world rejects, the church exalts. The world did not, and does not, know that it needed God to become a man and bear our sins by dying the death of an outcast traitor. Yet this is the heart of Christianity! So if a church begins to peddle a message that pleases the world, of course the true gospel will be de-emphasized, compromised, even replaced.

⊙ Apply

Do you expect the world to think you wise, or foolish?

Are you prepared for people to be offended by what you believe about the cross?

Remember Humility

Read 1 Corinthians 1 v 26-31

What does your culture say are the most important qualities in someone?

What does you culture say it is acceptable to boast about?

In Corinth, status came from being known as wise, or powerful, or from a good family.

What status did the church members have (v 26)?

Why did God choose to make them his people (v 27-29)?

So what is the only thing a Christian can say is great, i.e. boast about (v 31)?

When your boasting is only about what someone else has done—how the Lord Jesus has died for you—it is hard to get proud and defensive and divisive.

⊙ Pray

Thank God for choosing you, through no merit or achievement of your own. Then speak to him about ways you find it hard to accept foolishness and remember humility.

~ Notes and Prayers ~

_____

_____

_____

_____

_____

_____

_____

_____

_____

_____

_____

_____

_____

_____

_____

_____

_____

_____

_____

_____

_____

_____

Nothing Except...

1 Corinthians 2 v 1-16

Paul practiced what he preached... or rather, we should say, he preached what he wrote.

When I Came

Read 1 Corinthians 2 v 1-5

In Paul's time, secular orators would come to Corinth, praise the city, tell of their achievements, and impress with their eloquence.

How was Paul somewhat different (v 1, 3)?!

What did Paul think was most important about his speaking (v 2)?

Why did he not want to seem impressive himself (v 5)?

⊙ Apply

How should we apply Paul's words here to our attitude to preachers today, do you think?

How do these verses encourage our own efforts to tell people about Jesus?

Imagine you found yourself moving to another community and looking for a new church.

What should you look for most of all?

A Message of Wisdom

Read 1 Corinthians 2 v 6-16

Paul has already said that the message at the heart of Christianity seems "foolishness" (1 v 18). Yet, at the same time, it is "a message of wisdom" (2 v 6)!

Who recognizes this (v 6)?

Who doesn't? How do we know this (v 8)?

So how can anyone see that trusting in the cross is true wisdom (v 10, 12)?

God's wisdom is a gift. And the ability to understand it is, too. People, including us, are by nature blind to the beauty of God's truth (v 14)—and so we need it to be revealed to us. Remembering this keeps us humble; and it reminds us that to the watching world, Christians will always seem odd.

⊙ Apply

Do you ever ignore God's wisdom because the world says it is foolish? How?

Do you find yourself listening to the world's wisdom even when you know God has said it is foolish? How?

How do these verses encourage you to live more by God's wisdom, and less by the world's?

⊙ Pray

Thank God for revealing the message of his Son crucified to you, through the work of his Spirit.

Pray that you would be able to judge everything in line with the Spirit's guidance; and that you would not be too concerned with the judgment of the world (v 16).

~ Notes and Prayers ~

Day
14

You Need to Grow Up!

1 Corinthians 3 v 1-23

If the apostle Paul were commenting on your Christian maturity, how would he describe you?

Children

Read 1 Corinthians 3 v 1-4

How does Paul describe the Corinthians (v 1-2)?

What proves that they are like this (v 3-4)?

Paul is writing to them as children because they just don't seem ready for anything more. And this is their fault. They had had every opportunity to grow in Christ— Paul had lived among them, and Peter (i.e. Cephas) seems to have visited them (1 v 12). Paul is not asking, spiritually speaking, a three-year-old to hold an adult conversation; he is asking a 33-year-old to move on to proper food.

⊙ Apply

Are you growing in Christian love, knowledge, obedience, godliness... in other words, Christian maturity?

Looking back over the last couple of years, how have you been growing?

Looking forward, in what areas do you need to "grow up"? What will you do in order to mature?

The Seed

Read 1 Corinthians 3 v 5-9

What does Paul teach us about Christian ministry here?

How is this reassuring? How is it humbling?

The Building

Read 1 Corinthians 3 v 10-17

God is the one who directs the various workmen he employs, because the church is his. And a true church is built on the foundation of Jesus Christ (v 11). God owns the church; and God lives in the church (v 16-17).

How will "church work" be judged (v 12-15)?

⊘ Apply

How should this affect our attitude toward our local church? And toward our work for our church?

All is Yours

Read 1 Corinthians 3 v 18-23

How is verse 21 a summary of Paul's argument through chapters 2 and 3?

A mature Christian realizes there's no need for division in a church; no need to seek reflected glory by backing a particular pastor or speaker or organization.

Why? Because everything God has promised is already theirs, not through following Paul, Apollos or Cephas, but by belonging to Christ (v 22-23). While worldly wisdom tells us to put ourselves forward, godly wisdom urges us to enjoy all we have in Jesus, and exalt him.

⊙ Pray

Praise God now for giving you real life, no fear of death, and a place in his world to come.

~ Notes and Prayers ~

_____
_____
_____
_____
_____
_____
_____
_____
_____
_____
_____
_____
_____
_____
_____
_____
_____
_____
_____
_____
_____

Day
15

Real or Fake?
Part One

1 Corinthians 4 v 1-7

Little destroys a church faster than false teaching. Paul knew the Corinthian Christians were being fooled, misled and deceived by imposters. The danger is no less real for churches today.

But how do you spot the real and the fake? Paul gives us four marks of a real Christian minister. We'll see two in this section, and two in the next.

Read 1 Corinthians 4 v 1-7

The Message

What have ministers been given (v 1)?

What must they do with this (v 2)?

Read 1 Corinthians 2 v 1-2

What is the "secret" ministers are to reveal to people?

Ministers are stewards of God's message. They are not owners; they've been entrusted with someone else's property. They are God's employees; and they work for him. And reliability is what he wants, more than originality.

What mistake does Paul warn ministers against in 4 v 6?

Why might it be tempting for a minister to ignore this warning?

Here's the first mark of a true Christian minister: *he preaches a cross-centered message.* No less, and no more.

Whose Opinion?

Whose judgment does Paul care about (v 4)?

What is this judgment concerned with, and when will it happen (v 5)?

What impact does this have on his view of other people's opinions of him (v 3)?

A true minister of Christ (and every true Christian, for that matter) lives to please Christ. It is his praise, and his judgment, that are all that matters. He knows the gospel message will not always be popular. He knows it will never score highly in opinion polls and focus groups.

But he is not ultimately answerable to the world, or even to his church, but to God, who has entrusted him with the message of the cross.

There is actually great freedom here, for all Christians. We know the identity of our ultimate judge. We know that with him, there is "no condemnation for those who are in Christ Jesus" (Romans 8 v 1). And we know that he rewards our work for him (1 Corinthians 3 v 14). So we are free from being driven and dictated to by other people's opinions.

Here is the second mark of a true Christian minister: *he cares only about God's judgment of him.* No one else's.

⊙ Apply

When do you most need to remember this truth for yourself?

⊙ Pray

Pray for your church's leaders in the ways that this passage has prompted you to.

~ Notes and Prayers ~

_____

_____

_____

_____

_____

_____

_____

_____

_____

_____

_____

_____

_____

_____

_____

_____

_____

_____

_____

_____

_____

_____

Real or Fake?
Part Two

1 Corinthians 4 v 8-21

A real gospel minister preaches only a cross-shaped message, and cares only about God's judgment. Now here are two more marks of the sort of ministers that God likes, and that we need.

The Life they Lead

Read 1 Corinthians 4 v 8-13

Paul uses very sharp, ironic comments here, to deflate the Corinthians' pride in themselves.

How does he (sarcastically) describe them (v 8, 10)?

Clearly, many in the Corinthian church were feeling confident and fulfilled. It seems the false teachers were telling them, *You're great! You can have it all!*

How does Paul (without sarcasm) describe himself (v 10-13)?

What point is he making about the Christian life, do you think?

In first-century military processions (v 9), the prisoners came last in line, and very last of all came the lowest in rank. This, Paul says, is his experience of life; very different to having "begun to reign" (v 8)!

But this is the Christian life: because it was Christ's life. Paul would have been an embarrassment to well-to-do Corinthian citizens. But true ministers of Christ are happy to be despised, happy to sacrifice anything, if in so doing the gospel is displayed.

The third mark of a real minister is: *he lives a cross-centered lifestyle.*

What do you really want from your pastor? Someone respectable, polite, who your non-Christian friends warm to? Or someone who is willing to give up his wealth, comfort and reputation in order to teach Christ?

The Followers they Form

Read 1 Corinthians 4 v 14-21

How does Paul describe his relationship with these Christians (v 14-15)?

What does Paul want his "children" to do (v 16)?

A Christian minister is called not only to teach the gospel correctly, live in sight of Christ's judgment, and live a Christlike life. He is also—the fourth mark—*to urge others to do the same.*

⊘ Apply

Paul was the one who had first told them the gospel. There is (or should be!) a special regard for those whom God has used to lead us to Christ.

Why not get in touch today with the person or people who first told you about Jesus, and thank them?

⊙ Pray

It is not easy being a faithful minister. Pray for yours now: that they would continue to grow in all four areas of true gospel ministry. And pray that you would allow them to challenge you to live a more cross-centered life!

~ Notes and Prayers ~

Dealing with Sin

1 Corinthians 5 v 1-5

Judgmentalism. It's something Christians are often accused of, and never want to be guilty of. But does this mean that we can never think that something is wrong? Or that if something is wrong, we must never do anything about it?

In a world where we're told the only judgment that counts is your own, we need to be helped, and challenged, by chapters 5 and 6 of this letter.

Read 1 Corinthians 5 v 1-5

The Situation

What was going on in this congregation (v 1)?

How had the church responded to this (v 2)?

It's an error to judge by standards that God has not revealed. But it's no less an error not to judge by standards that God has revealed. And, just as the pagan world had decided (v 1), the Bible is clear that incest is wrong, and brings judgment (e.g. Deuteronomy 22 v 30).

The Right Solution

So, what should the Corinthian Christians have done (1 Corinthians 5 v 2)?

Notice that Paul has already determined the truth, and given judgment on, this situation. There are things which God has said are wrong—sinful—regardless of the circumstances.

Does other Christians' sin cause you to "[go] into mourning"? If not, why not?

Paul describes excommunication as "hand[ing] this man over to Satan" (v 5). By this, he means the church removing their affirmation of his salvation, his belonging to God. Excommunication isn't an announcement that someone is definitely not a Christian; it is a recognition that they are not living as a Christian, and therefore have chosen not to be treated as a Christian. Excommunication would not necessarily have forbidden the man to attend public services; but he wouldn't have been able to share the Lord's Supper.

What was the aim of this excommunication (v 5)?

It is very hard to deal with sin that is never mentioned, never exposed, never challenged. Excommunication shows that sin is sin; and that sin is serious; and Paul is praying that the shock of it will bring this man to realize it, to turn away from his sinful nature and back to his Lord who stands ready to forgive.

⊙ Apply

Is there any sin that you know has taken root in your life, which you're not dealing with?

What do you need to do about it?

Who will you ask for support from?

Is there anyone you know who needs to have their sin, lovingly but firmly, pointed out to them?

~ Notes and Prayers ~

_____

_____

_____

_____

_____

_____

_____

_____

_____

_____

_____

_____

_____

_____

_____

_____

_____

_____

_____

_____

_____

_____

Day
18

The Problem
with Yeast

1 Corinthians 5 v 6-13

In the previous passage, we saw Paul calling for the church to discipline a man for his own good. But it's not only him who is affected by his sin...

Which Bread?

Read 1 Corinthians 5 v 6-8

The man who is a sexual sinner is the "yeast." So what point is Paul making in verse 6?

So what do they need to do as a church, and why (v 7a)?

At the Passover, all yeast was removed from Jewish homes (see Exodus 12 v 15). But the Passover was always pointing forward to the ultimate Lamb—to Jesus, who died to rescue his people from sin and death. Christ's death establishes the church; the church now needs to "keep the Festival" by excluding wickedness and upholding sincerity and truth" (1 Corinthians 5 v 8).

Notice that it's not the man's sin, so much as the church's indifference to (and even boasting about) it that has Paul yelling here. Sin is an infection that will spread among those who tolerate it. Sin that no one deals with becomes sin that everyone will have to deal with.

What are the sins that your church would be most likely to tolerate?

Whose Business?

Read 1 Corinthians 5 v 9-13

What command does Paul underline in verse 9?

What doesn't he mean by this (v 10)? So what does he mean (v 11)?

What principle does he set down in verses 12-13?

Perhaps it is fair to say that often, the church is very quick to pass judgment on ethical misconduct of the outside community, while being very slow to address flaws in the conduct of its members. Paul, on the other hand, leaves the world to God. His concern is with the church: that this church takes sin seriously, and pursues purity properly.

Why do we often get this the wrong way around, do you think?

What does verse 11 look like in practice? I think it means not acting in any way that will cause the person who is sinning to think that their lifestyle doesn't matter. We're not called to shun them completely; but things like eating with them would suggest that we still see them as a member of Christ's church, regardless of their rejection of his Lordship.

⊙ Pray

These issues are not easy. Thank God that Christ the Lamb has died for your church's sins. Thank him that he cares about your conduct. Ask him to help you to take purity seriously, and to help others to do so, too, even when that is unpopular.

~ Notes and Prayers ~

Day
19

Courting
Disaster

1 Corinthians 6 v 1-11

Paul wants Christians to judge Christianly: for the sakes of sinning members, of the church as a whole... and the sake of society.

Read 1 Corinthians 6 v 1-8

On Show

What is happening between church members (v 1, 6)?

What does Paul suggest is the problem with doing this (end of v 6)?

What extra details about the Christians' behavior does v 8 add?

Why would all this be a terrible witness to non-Christians?

Paul reminds these Christians that, one day, they will sit with Christ and judge the whole world (v 2). Surely they can sort out their own petty disputes without parading their divisions in front of the watching world, which would love an excuse not to take the gospel seriously!

Why Not?

What should their attitude be instead (v 7)?

This is not just, *Don't do wrong*. This is, *Be willing to be wronged, if it helps your witness to outsiders*. Better to be cheated out of what you deserve than to risk damaging the reputation and witness of your church.

Paul is not talking here about covering up illegal acts. He calls these disputes "trivial" (v 2)—petty arguments which have escalated into court cases. These verses are not a wall behind which criminal acts in churches can be hidden.

⊙ Apply

What would need to change in your own heart for you to be more content to be wrongly treated, and not need to get your own back?

What Some of you Were

Read 1 Corinthians 6 v 9-11

What is the warning in these verses (v 9-10)?

If a church isn't willing to call these things sinful, and act to make sure they are not part of church life, what will the impact be on:

• *Christians struggling against these sins?*
• *Christians who have given in to these sins?*

Why is verse 11 such good news?

There is no sin that the Lord Jesus cannot cover. One reason the gospel is offensive is because Jesus forgives things that society will not. But the gospel does not only hold out forgiveness: it commands change. What we were is not who we are.

⊙ Pray

What has the Lord Jesus forgiven you?

Thank him!

How has the Spirit of God changed you?

Praise him!

Where do you need him to continue to change you?

Ask him!

~ Notes and Prayers ~

_____

_____

_____

_____

_____

_____

_____

_____

_____

_____

_____

_____

_____

_____

_____

_____

_____

_____

_____

_____

_____

_____

Day

20

Body Matters

1 Corinthians 6 v 12-20

Paul now gives one final reason why sin, and particularly sexual sin, needs to be called sin, and dealt with as sin, by the individual and by the church.

What is the Body for?

Read 1 Corinthians 6 v 12-15a

In verses 12 and 13 Paul is apparently quoting two of the popular but false slogans that were circulating at the time. The context here is sex, not eating!

So what attitude towards sex do the two sayings seem to be promoting?

What is Paul's answer to this (v 13b-15a)?

Paul is countering the idea that it's our spirit that really counts; so it doesn't matter what we do with our bodies. The Lord Jesus was raised physically; so will we be. Our bodies will live eternally, and belong to God eternally. God cares about what we do with our bodies.

What does Sex do?

Read 1 Corinthians 6 v 15b-17

What happens when someone sleeps with a prostitute (v 16)?

What is Paul telling us about sex here?

And, since there is no division between who we are spiritually and what we do physically, we cannot both be united with the Lord through faith (v 17) while uniting ourselves sexually with anyone we're not married to (v 16).

⊙ Apply

Are you struggling with sexual sin in some way (in your mind as well as with your body)?

Will you admit it to yourself, get help if you need it, and ask the Lord for forgiveness and cleansing?

Always remember, "You were washed, you were sanctified, you were justified in the name of our Lord Jesus Christ" (v 11). There is no sin that the Lord does not care about; there is no sin that the Lord cannot cleanse us of.

What your Body is

Read 1 Corinthians 6 v 18-20

How is a Christian's body described (v 19)?

It cost a great price to make our bodies homes of the living God: the price of his Son's blood. God has made us, and God has bought us. Now we are to live to bring honor to him.

We do not glorify God with our bodies by burnishing and polishing them at the gym until they shine; we do it by using our bodies relationally and sexually in the ways he commands in his word.

⊙ Apply

Who do you view your body as belonging to? Is it yours? Or is it God's?

"You were bought at a price" (v 20).

How will this make a difference to how you use your body?

~ Notes and Prayers ~

Day

21

Situational Service

1 Corinthians 7 v 17-24, 29-31

Chapter 7 deals with some hard issues: marriage, sex, singleness. But above all, it deals with circumstances: and how Christians should view them.

What types of circumstances are people around you working to gain, or to keep? How about you?

How important are your circumstances to how content you feel?

Most people today think that worldly circumstances are all-important. The key to solving our problems, and to gaining the life we'd like, must therefore be achieved by changing our circumstances. So we confidently, restlessly, sometimes even desperately, act to change our situations.

Read 1 Corinthians 7 v 17-24, 29-31

Called by God...

Paul repeatedly raises the idea of "calling" in these verses. He's making the point that there is something that matters more than our circumstances, and that is our relationship with God.

In verse 22, what does Paul call slaves? What does he call those who are free?

By "reversing" the "status" of these two groups, what point is he making?

All Christians are, in fact, both! We are called by God to serve Christ and obey him as our Master; and we are called by God to enjoy the freedom of knowing life as we were meant to live it, for ever.

What do we know about all our present circumstances (v 31)?

How does Paul describe "the time" we live in, between Jesus' resurrection and return (v 29)?

The Christian knows that the future matters more than the present. It is better than even the best of circumstances now; and it lasts infinitely longer! We live with the light of the future streaming back into the present, which rearranges our priorities in the here and now.

... To Serve God

God has called us to know him.

What else has he called us to (v 24)?

Our job is not primarily to seek to change our circumstances, so much as to seek to serve Christ in and through our circumstances.

⊙ Apply

Are your prayers more about changing your situation, or about being able to live for Christ in your situation?

When do you find it hardest to remember your calling matters more than your circumstances? How could you remind yourself that you have been freed to enjoy serving Christ?

What circumstances in your life would you not have chosen? How could you use those circumstances to serve the Lord Jesus?

~ Notes and Prayers ~

_____
_____
_____
_____
_____
_____
_____
_____
_____
_____
_____
_____
_____
_____
_____
_____
_____
_____
_____
_____
_____
_____

Day
22

The Ins and Outs of Marriage

1 Corinthians 7 v 1-16

These verses contain the most direct, extensive teaching on marriage in the whole of the Bible.

Read 1 Corinthians 7 v 1-16

Being Married

In verse 1, Paul is probably quoting from what the Corinthians "wrote about" in a letter to him. It seems some of them thought sex and marriage were somehow un-spiritual—not right for Christians who are looking forward to Jesus' return.

What answer does Paul give (v 1-5)?

Why is it good to be married (v 2, 5)?

Verse 4 would have been counter-cultural in Corinth, and still is today. Sex is a way to give, not to get; primarily a way to honor another, not to bring pleasure to ourselves. God created sex to be given within marriage; our greatest satisfaction— even sexually—will come in bringing satisfaction to our spouse.

Ending Marriage?

Tragically, though God created marriage to be lifelong, in this imperfect world that doesn't always happen. All our marriages can only be "till death do us part"; and some end before that, in divorce.

How does Paul tell Christians to deal with these different situations:

• *Considering ending a marriage (v 10-11)?*
• *A Christian who has a non-Christian spouse (v 12-14)?*
• *A Christian whose non-Christian spouse leaves them (v 15-16)?*
• *A widow (or widower) (see v 39-40)?*

Verse 14 is not saying that an unbelieving husband is saved simply because his wife has faith. Paul is saying only that God regards such a marriage as legitimate, and the children of such a marriage as legitimate.

But in verse 16, Paul does point out that remaining in such a marriage might bring the spouse to faith. This is not an excuse for Christians thinking of entering marriage with a non-Christian (v 39 shows that is wrong). But it does give hope to a Christian in an existing marriage with a non-Christian.

Where would your society agree with the Bible's teaching here? Where would it differ?

⊙ Apply

Are there any ways this passage is prodding you to change your attitude, or actions, or decisions? How are you going to respond?

⊙ Pray

Thank God for marriage, and for the joy of selfless sex within marriage.

Pray for those (perhaps yourself) whose marriages are difficult. Ask God to give them patience and godliness. Ask him to work in those marriages (perhaps your own) to bring belief to the unbelieving and healing to the hurting.

~ Notes and Prayers ~

_____

_____

_____

_____

_____

_____

_____

_____

_____

_____

_____

_____

_____

_____

_____

_____

_____

_____

_____

_____

_____

_____

Day
23

The Single Issue

1 Corinthians 7 v 7-9, 25-38

Our culture doesn't know what to make of singleness. On one hand, it is lauded as offering "freedom." On the other (and particularly for women) there is a notion that something has gone wrong if you have no-one to come home to... What does the Bible say about being single?

A Gift

Read 1 Corinthians 7 v 7-9

Paul was himself single.

So what is he saying about singleness here?

Can that really be right?!

Three Reasons

Read 1 Corinthians 7 v 25-38

Here, Paul gives three reasons why it is good not to marry—to be single.

First, how does Paul describe marriage in verse 28?! What aspects of marriage do you think he has in mind here?

Second, Paul says believers are free to pass on marriage because it is part of this world, and "this world in its present form is passing away" (v 31). There will be no human marriage in eternal life to come (Luke 20 v 34-36). The circumstances of this world are not permanent.

What is the third reason Paul gives that Christian singleness is good (v 32-35)?

Christians are free. We are free to be married, and there are good reasons to be so. And we are free not to be married—and there are good reasons for this, too. Both circumstances are gifts from the Lord (v 7), which we can use to serve him (remember verse 24?). Because this world is passing away, what matters most is not whether there is a ring on our finger, but whether we have been called into a perfect eternity by God.

One more thing: we need to be clear that Paul is not teaching asceticism—that to be holy, we must deny ourselves worldly pleasures. After all, he commands sex between spouses (v 3)! Any preference Paul has for singleness is not rooted in a desire to deny pleasure, but rather to encourage God-centeredness.

⊙ Apply

If you are married...

Do you, and does your church, subconsciously suggest that marriage is better than single-ness, perhaps with the topics of your conversations; how you spend your leisure time; what events the church organizes?

If you are single...

What opportunities does your singleness give you to serve God? Are you using your circumstances to live for Jesus, or thinking, "I'll find a spouse, and then love and serve God"?

⊙ Pray

Pray for yourself and for your friends: that you would use your circumstances to serve God, and help others around you to do the same.

~ Notes and Prayers ~

○
Day
24

Use Knowledge
Lovingly

1 Corinthians 8 v 1-13

What are your most important rights?

Would anything cause you to give them up?

I n Corinth, animal sacrifices were a regular part of pagan worship; and meat sold in the markets often came from sacrifices offered in pagan temples. Anyone eating such meat, either at home or at a feast in a pagan temple, might be considered a worshiper of that "god."

What we Know

Read 1 Corinthians 8 v 4-8

What do Christians "know" about God and about idols (v 4-6)?

And what do they know about food (v 8)?

So the believers in Corinth were free to eat meat sacrificed to idols.

But... what did some Christians believe (v 7)?

And it is a dangerous thing to go against our conscience, even where our conscience is misinformed. For a Christian who saw the food as sinful to eat, it was sinful to eat.

How we Love

Read 1 Corinthians 8 v 1-3 and 9-13

Knowledge alone makes us proud (v 1). But if we know God, we will love God (v 2-3)—and this will make us humble and loving towards others, seeking their good (v 1).

Remember, it is not wrong to eat meat sacrificed to idols.

But in what circumstances would it be wrong (v 10-12)?

The "weak brother or sister" might be led to sin against their own conscience; or to think that sin doesn't matter at all, and so sin in other ways. He or she will be "destroyed" (v 11).

Far better for the knowledgeable Christian to give up their right to eat this meat, than for them to insist on their right to enjoy the meat, and in doing so lead a weaker believer to sin. In fact, to insist on their rights instead of doing what's best for other Christians is, itself, sinful (v 12). It is possible to do something that is not in itself sinful in an unthinking, unhelpful way that makes it sinful.

On the one hand, we need to educate our consciences with the Bible. But, on the other, we need to be willing to give up what we're free to do if that helps others.

⊙ Apply

Christians are free to drink alcohol; to wear make-up; to dress (within reason) as we like; to buy a brand new car.

In what circumstances would it be loving not to exercise each of those rights around other Christians?

Is there anything you are doing that might be a "stumbling block" to another Christian? What will you do about this?

~ Notes and Prayers ~

_____
_____
_____
_____
_____
_____
_____
_____
_____
_____
_____
_____
_____
_____
_____
_____
_____
_____
_____
_____
_____
_____

Rights Used Rightly

1 Corinthians 9 v 1-18

Paul doesn't just preach giving up our rights for the sake of the church. He practices it, too...

Paul's Rights

Read 1 Corinthians 9 v 1-11

What proves that Paul is a true apostle, chosen by God to speak with God's authority (v 1-2)?

What does he have the right to do, as an apostle (v 5-6)?

In verses 7-12, Paul is simply underlining why he has these rights. It's the way the human world works (v 7-8). But it's also how God wants the world to work; since he wants oxen to be rewarded for their work (v 9, quoting Deuteronomy 25 v 4), he wants people to be rewarded, too (v 10). So, as Paul the church-planting apostle sows spiritual seed, he is entitled to material pay by those churches (v 11).

Paul's Use of his Rights

Read 1 Corinthians 9 v 12-18

No sooner has Paul established his right to support than he does what (v 12, 15)?

But "the Lord has commanded that those who preach the gospel should [have the right to] receive their living from the gospel" (v 14).

So why did Paul "not use" it, does he suggest (v 12, 17-18)?

Paul did use his right to be supported by the churches elsewhere (e.g. Philippians 4 v 15-16); so why not here? Perhaps he wanted to distance himself from the orators whose whole aim in speaking was to earn money, whose message came at a price. He wanted to make sure no one thought the gospel offer was not free, that they had to buy their forgiveness (v 18). The freedom of belonging to God as part of his people did come at a price; but the price has been paid by God, not the Christian (6 v 20).

So in Corinth, Paul has given up his rights to support so that no one, Christian or non-believer, will misunderstand his message. Christ has paid the cost to offer forgiveness for free; Paul will pay a cost to preach that message for free. He gives up his rights to make sure the gospel is easily seen and understood.

⊘ Pray

Thank God for those who were willing to risk giving up their freedom to enjoy safety, material comforts, or popularity, to preach the gospel to you.

⊘ Apply

Re-read 1 Corinthians 6 v 6-11

How does the gospel message itself motivate you to share it with others, even though that comes at a cost of some kind to you?

How can your actions today display the truth that God loves people at great cost to himself, and without cost to them?

~ Notes and Prayers ~

_____
_____
_____
_____
_____
_____
_____
_____
_____
_____
_____
_____
_____
_____
_____
_____
_____
_____
_____
_____
_____
_____
_____
_____

All Things to All People

1 Corinthians 9 v 19-22

I t wasn't only in Corinth that Paul was willing to give up what he was free to enjoy, for the sake of others.

Paul's Example

Read 1 Corinthians 9 v 19-22

What does Paul do (v 19)? What does this mean in day-to-day life, do you think?

Why does Paul do this (v 19)?

How does he act as a slave to Jews (v 20)?

Paul is not implying that he has placed himself back under Old Testament law because he is looking to his obedience to make him right with God. He is saying that he adopts all the customs and rituals of Jewish cultural life. This is astonishing!

It was these customs that Paul had once relied on for salvation, and which Christ had saved him from. Yet he's willing to follow them once more, "so as to win those under the law" (v 20). Paul says he has "become all things to all people" (v 22).

Apart from living as a Jew when he's among Jews, what else has this meant for him (v 21-22)?

⊙ Apply

What different worldviews and belief systems do people who live around you hold to?

What kind of lifestyle and behavior would a Christian need to have in order to get along-side them?

How would the gospel message be "good news" for those people?

Christ's Attitude

Read Philippians 2 v 5-11

What rights did Christ have (v 6)?

What did he do with those rights (v 6-8)?

At the heart of the gospel message we meet God the Son, who was free to reign in glory in heaven, and yet who chose to die on a cross to suffer the death of sinners.

How in 1 Corinthians 9 do we see Paul obeying what he writes in Philippians 2 v 5?

⊙ Apply

Do you have any rights that you are not really willing to give up for the sake of others? Perhaps:

- *weekends, or Sunday evenings?*

- *time with your friends?*

- *a particular kind of music?*

- *your home country, or large house?*

- *your holidays?*

- *doing what you want, when you want?*

⊙ Pray

Ask God to give you a heart full of humble, self-giving, encouraging love.

Ask him to enable you to follow the example of Paul, and have the attitude of Christ, so that you will inconvenience yourself to make the gospel known to others.

~ Notes and Prayers ~

_____

_____

_____

_____

_____

_____

_____

_____

_____

_____

_____

_____

_____

_____

_____

_____

_____

_____

_____

_____

_____

_____

_____

_____

Day
27

Strict
Training

1 Corinthians 9 v 23-27

When it comes to sacrificing his rights, Paul does "all this for the sake of the gospel" (v 23). But it's for his own sake, too...

Read 1 Corinthians 9 v 23-27

The Prize

How does Paul picture the Christian life (v 24)?

The Isthmian Games, held near Corinth, were famous all over the Roman world. The winner of each race received a victory wreath made of small pine branches.

What contrast does Paul draw (v 25)?

Paul's point is, If it's worth going into "strict training" for such a prize, how much more seriously should we take reaching the finishing line "to get a crown that will last forever"?!

What does "strict training" look like (v 27)?

When Paul talks about his body in this way, he probably has in mind the danger in Corinth of believers giving in to sexual temptation, and using their bodies to disobey God (as he's written to them about in chapters 5 and 6).

⊘ Apply

How do you find it hardest to master your body, instead of allowing it to master you?

What "strict training" do you need to undergo?

How will verse 25 motivate you?

Don't get Disqualified!

What does Paul think is a possibility for him, even though he is preaching about the heavenly crown to others (v 27)?

Paul has been urging the Corinthians to give up their rights in order to live and share the gospel message. But verse 27 reminds us that it is not preaching the gospel that saves us: it is trusting in it. It is not talking about Jesus as Lord that wins us the prize: it is treating him as Lord. It is a huge encouragement to know that the prize we speak about is the prize that we are headed for; but it is hugely sobering to remember that we can "be disqualified" by not continuing to live with Jesus Christ as our Lord, even as we continue to talk about him to others.

⊘ Apply

Do you need to hear the challenge in verse 27 today? How?

⊘ Pray

Pray for your church leaders: that they will stay in strict training themselves, following Jesus as Lord even as they teach you to.

~ Notes and Prayers ~

_____

_____

_____

_____

_____

_____

_____

_____

_____

_____

_____

_____

_____

_____

_____

_____

_____

_____

_____

_____

Warnings from the Past

1 Corinthians 10 v 1-13

Paul has told the Corinthians to follow his example, making sure their bodies serve their God, rather than becoming their god. Now, he gives them an example not to follow...

Read 1 Corinthians 10 v 1-11

Blessings in the Desert

Paul looks back to the Old Testament, to Israel's exodus from Egypt. These people are Christians' spiritual "forefathers."

How had they known great blessing (v 1-4)?

"Baptized into Moses" means they had followed Moses' leadership, and were delivered by God through his leadership.

If you have time, read about these blessings in more detail in Exodus 14 v 21-31; 16 v 4-5; 17 v 5-6.

Bodies in the Desert

So why is verse 5 such a shock?

Verses 6-11 explain why verse 5 happened. Paul gives four specific reasons for God's reaction to this most blessed generation.

Pick out the first two in verses 7 and 8.

The third sin of the Israelites was that some of them decided to "test the Lord" (v 9, NIV84) or "test Christ" (NIV2011). The scholar D.A. Carson defines this as "chronic and repeated unbelief with attitudes": seeing how much sin we can get away with.

What is the fourth (v 10)?

This is not an emotional state, or a onetime complaint. It's an open distrust, the settled opinion that we would do a better job than God.

Why is Paul mentioning all this to the Corinthians (v 11)?

The Old Testament is not *only* an example to us: it also points us to Christ, who he is and why he came. But it is never *less* than an example to us.

Standing Firm?

Read 1 Corinthians 10 v 12-13

What is the warning that Paul draws from the example of our "forefathers" (v 12)?

Why is complacency so dangerous to Christians and churches, do you think?

⊙ Apply

Look back to the four ways Israel were disobedient. Which of these are you most likely to fall into?

Do you need to do something about a sin you are failing to deal with?

Are you in danger of thinking that baptism, church attendance or taking communion mean you are right with God?

Remember that it is only trusting in, and seeking to be obedient to, Christ that saves you!

~ Notes and Prayers ~

_____

_____

_____

_____

_____

_____

_____

_____

_____

_____

_____

_____

_____

_____

_____

_____

_____

_____

_____

_____

_____

_____

_____

Day
29

Free from Idolatry

1 Corinthians 10 v 14-22

What the Christians in Corinth ate didn't matter. But *where* they ate did matter a great deal.

The Principle

Read 1 Corinthians 10 v 14 and 22

The command is clear: Flee false gods!

Notice the "therefore" in verse 14. How is the instruction of this verse a consequence of what we saw in the last study?

How does verse 22 underline the importance of making sure we don't worship false gods?

Jealousy is not the same as envy. Envy is wanting something that is rightfully someone else's. Jealousy is wanting something that is rightfully yours. God deserves to be treated as God; nothing else does. When people worship something he has made, instead of worshiping him, he is right to be jealous.

In Practice

Read 1 Corinthians 10 v 15-21

Paul is talking here about eating at the great public feasts in Corinth, which were held in pagan temples. The meat there had been publicly offered to the pagan "gods." The social and political life of the city was centered on these feasts. It would be hard to not eat there.

What does Paul say about idols (v 19)?

So what is the problem with eating at the pagan temples (v 20)?

Western societies today may not worship statues, but they still treat created things as what they need to give them a fulfilling, secure life—as idols.

What are the most common idols in your culture?

What does verse 20 tell us about what is really going on when our culture worships something as a "god"?

A Different Meal

Paul contrasts these pagan feasts with another feast.

What does he tell us about the Lord's Supper (v 16-17)?

Paul doesn't mean that the bread and the wine become Christ himself in some way. He is thinking of the effect of sharing them. To receive the cup and bread rightly—with faith—is to receive Christ, to share in the benefits of his death. Taking the Lord's Supper doesn't save us. Trusting in the death of Christ that is proclaimed in the Lord's Supper does.

Ultimately, what choice do the Corinthians have to make (v 21)?

⊙ Apply

We either seek to worship the Lord Jesus, and flee our idols; or we worship our idols, and flee the Lord Jesus. There is no middle ground. So ask yourself:

What do I think about and talk about most? What most excites me?

Your answer is a good indication of what you're most tempted to make an idol of—and a crucial thing to pray about now.

~ Notes and Prayers ~

_____
_____
_____
_____
_____
_____
_____
_____
_____
_____
_____
_____
_____
_____
_____
_____
_____
_____
_____
_____
_____

Day

30

Liberty, Legalism and Love

1 Corinthians 10 v 23 – 11 v 1

These verses are a summary of Paul's teaching in chapters 8 – 10. They help us to avoid being directed by our liberty—what we're free to do. And they free us from being dictated to by legalism—rules about what we mustn't do.

Liberty

Read 1 Corinthians 10 v 23-26

In verse 23, Paul is again quoting the chants used by some of the Corinthians.

How does he agree with them (v 25-26)?

Even if it has been previously offered to a false god, the Corinthian Christians are at liberty to enjoy eating anything and everything God has given them.

Liberty Limited

Read 1 Corinthians 10 v 27-29a

When should the Corinthians not eat the meat that they are free to eat (v 28)?!

Paul wants these Christians to determine their actions by what would be of most help to their non-Christian friends. In this situation, eating the meat might confuse an unbeliever about the gospel. They might think Christianity includes idol worship; that Jesus is just one more addition to the long list of pagan gods.

When we have settled in our minds that something is not wrong—that we have liberty to do it—we must still think about whether the action is right or wrong in a particular circumstance.

Avoiding Legalism

Read 1 Corinthians 10 v 29b-30

A legalistic response to this situation would be simply to make a rule that eating meat from the market is wrong. But Paul resists this. If he eats the meat "with thankfulness," why should he be "denounced" (v 30)? After all, meat is a gift from God (v 26)!

The Way of Love

Read 1 Corinthians 10 v 31 – 11 v 1

What should we be seeking in everything we do (12 v 31)?

We do this by showing and telling the truth about him—how holy and pure and loving and kind he is.

What should we make sure we don't do (v 32)? Why (v 33)?

Our actions shouldn't be directed by our liberty to do them; or by legalistic rules; but by love. Love for God, and love for the lost.

⊙ Pray

Father, thank you that you have given me the freedom to enjoy the life you made me for, knowing your Son and living his way.

Help me to see how I can glorify you in every action today. Help me to see how I can make your gospel plain to others, in how I live as well as how I speak.

Please make your glory and their good my greatest aims in how I live today. Amen.

~ Notes and Prayers ~

Day
31

Called to Faith, Called to Change

1 Corinthians 1 – 11 (summary)

We have been moving quickly through this most challenging of New Testament epistles. And when we break a book of the Bible into small sections as we have done here, it is easy to forget the main thrust and overall arc of the teaching. So in this study, we are pausing to recap and reflect upon the emphases of Paul's writings in the first eleven chapters of this wonderful letter.

Who Paul was Writing to

Corinth, remember, was a busy trading city in Greece. Paul had planted a church there about three years before he wrote to them. Now, he was in Ephesus, in modern-day Turkey.

Look up these verses. What was the Corinthian church like?

• *1 v 11-12*
• *3 v 3*
• *4 v 18*
• *5 v 1-2*
• *6 v 6-7*
• *8 v 8-13*

In a few words, summarize how this church is doing.

What are the main issues your own church is facing?

Are there any ways in which the problems in this Corinthian church are seen in yours?

What Paul Wants to Say

Read 1 Corinthians 10 v 31 – 11 v 1

What did Paul want these Christians to think about as they went about their daily lives?

- *v 31*
- *v 32*
- *v 33b*

Whose ultimate example did he want them to follow (11 v 1)?

⊙ Apply

Which of these three motivations for life do you most often forget? What will change if you make an effort to remember that motivation?

Sinful yet Perfect

Read 1 Corinthians 1 v 26-31

How are the Corinthians described (v 26-27)?

What matters is not that they're impressive, wealthy or intelligent, but that God has "called" them (v 26).

What do they have because they are "in Christ Jesus" (v 30)?

This may be a messed-up, sinful church. But it is full of people who, though struggling, are perfect, pure and free because they have faith in Christ. Throughout this challenging letter, we need to remember that what matters most is that we have been called by God to be "in Christ Jesus"—and that in him, despite our failings, we have been made perfect.

⊙ Pray

Thank God for calling you to put your faith in Christ. Thank him for your righteousness, holiness, and redemption. Ask him to enable you to remember, and be changed by, all that you have been excited and challenged by so far in the letter.

~ Notes and Prayers ~

_____

_____

_____

_____

_____

_____

_____

_____

_____

_____

_____

_____

_____

_____

_____

_____

_____

_____

_____

_____

_____

_____

_____

_____

Day
32

Not Really About Hats

1 Corinthians 11 v 2-16

This is a famously difficult—and controversial—passage. So we're going to spend two studies looking at it...

Read 1 Corinthians 11 v 2-16

The words "man" and "woman" here also mean "husband" and "wife." I think that these verses were written with married couples uppermost in Paul's mind.

Who is the head of a man/husband (v 3)?

Who is the head of a woman/wife (v 3)?

Men and their Head

In Corinth, the most wealthy and respected men would pull over their heads a portion of their best toga when they led prayer in a pagan temple. This was a way of indicating their high social status—to point to themselves.

Why would a man who did this in church be "dishonor[ing] his head" (v 3-4)?

The last place in which money or other kinds of worldly status should be recognized is in a community of judgment-deserving, Christ-redeemed, grace-bought, Spirit-filled people—the church. Men with authority in a church need to point to *the* authority—their head, Christ.

Women and their Head

In those days, headgear and hairstyle reflected a woman's marital status. Covered hair showed you were married; if hair was uncovered and flowing, you were very much available.

So if a woman in the Corinthian church stood up "with her head uncovered" (v 5), what would she probably have been trying to do?

The attitudes that lie behind this behavior in Corinth have a devastating effect on a church. Outsiders are put off by the self-centeredness. Sexual immorality will become even more of a temptation (as happened in Corinth, see 5 v 1-2). And Christ—the true head of the church, the one whose authority and beauty we gather to praise—will not be glorified.

⊘ Apply

These days, men don't cover their heads to show how important they are! And women don't wear their hair uncovered and loose in order to make men think about how attractive they are.

So how would a desire to show off status or attractiveness show itself in a church today? Here are some possibilities for men:

• Deliberately wearing expensive clothing when leading a service.

• Mentioning a high-prestige job from the front.

• Using humor so that others will think you are funny.

And for women:

• Wearing clothing or make-up with the hope that men will notice and find you attractive.

• Acting in a way that makes men find you sexually interesting.

How might it look for you?

~ Notes and Prayers ~

God and Gender

1 Corinthians 11 v 2-16

What does your culture say is the difference between men and women?

Why is it easier to follow what the culture says than what the Bible says, if and where they differ?

Read 1 Corinthians 11 v 2-3, 11-16

Men and Women

What do verses 3-4 say about the relationship between men and women?

How do verses 11-12 balance this?

"Everything [i.e. both men and women] comes from God" (v 12). God has revealed something of himself, his nature and character, in creating two distinct sexes and in how they relate to each other. The church should not undermine this, but showcase it. One aspect of God's image, to be shown in men, is his loving authority. He is a leader and ruler, always doing what is best for those he leads. The other aspect, to be seen in women, is humble submission. We see both in God's Son, who loves and leads his church, but also submits to his Father and was humble enough to die.

The Bible teaches that there is no difference in value between men and women—both are made in God's image. But there is a difference in role—some things are reserved for women (e.g. childbirth), others for men (e.g. leading in marriage).

Cultures swing back and forth in their emphases, tending either to over-stress hierarchy (that men are to lead) or interdependence (that we need each other) and rarely keeping the two in balance. Churches will need sometimes to be refuges from exploitation and oppression, and sometimes from a refusal to see any difference between men and women.

Which of the two emphases does the society you live in currently emphasize?

How will this make it hard for you to live and speak as a Christian?

Glory and Disgrace

In verses 13-15, Paul says it is "a disgrace" for a man to have long hair, but "glory" for a woman. Again, we need to understand the culture of the time: long hair on a man denoted effeminacy—wanting to act like a woman. Long hair on women was considered particularly ladylike.

So what point do you think Paul is making about our attitude to our gender?

⊘ Pray

These are not easy or culturally acceptable ideas!

Thank God that he tells us how to live in his world, however much that world may disagree. Ask God to enable you to see how the truths here apply to your life and your church. Speak to God now about any issues raised in these verses which you're struggling with.

~ Notes and Prayers ~

Whose Supper?

1 Corinthians 11 v 17-34

Paul has more to say about the Corinthians and how they run their church services. Now he moves on to one of the central acts in any church—the Lord's Supper.

What is the point of the Lord's Supper (i.e. Communion), would you say?

My Meal

Read 1 Corinthians 11 v 17-22

What is shocking about what Paul says in verses 17 and 20?

What reasons does Paul give for his verdict on their services?

In Corinth, Sunday was a work day. So the wealthy church members could arrive at their gatherings before those who worked. Apparently, they were sharing a meal together, with those who arrived last—the poorest members—perhaps finding no food left, and the wealthier members drunk. The poorer Christians were being left out. Perhaps this was not deliberate—but it was thoughtless.

Read 1 Corinthians 10 v 17

How was the wealthier church members' behavior undermining part of the point of the Lord's Supper?

Our Meal

Read 1 Corinthians 11 v 33-34

What does Paul tell them to do instead?

⊙ Apply

In what ways could (or does) your church thoughtlessly cause divisions between richer and poorer members of the congregation?

How might you be doing this as an individual?

The Lord's Meal

Read 1 Corinthians 11 v 23-26

Why do all Christians need to share the Lord's Supper?

What do we remember as we eat the bread and drink the wine (v 24-25)?

What do we look forward to (v 26)?

The Lord's Supper, when properly celebrated, enables a church to stay united. It humbles us all, reminding us that we are all sinners, all needing Jesus' death in our place to be forgiven. We are all equal at the Lord's table.

It unites us, reminding us that Christ's death is the beginning and center of what makes us Christians. Whatever may make us different, we have something fundamental in common—Jesus died for us.

And it inspires us to love one another. It reminds us of Christ's sacrificial love—and moves us to love each other in the same way.

⊙ Apply

Next time you share the Lord's Supper, what will you think about?

How will you expect to feel as you take the bread and wine?

~ Notes and Prayers ~

Day
35

Preparing for Supper

1 Corinthians 11 v 23-32

Paul has challenged us not to be unthinking about others as we approach the Lord's Supper. Now, he challenges us again: don't be unthinking about yourself.

Prepare Properly

Read 1 Corinthians 11 v 23-29

What does Paul warn about in verse 27?

How does verse 29 help us to understand what Paul means by "an unworthy manner"?

Taking the Lord's Supper is not magic. It must be accompanied by faith, by recognizing that Jesus is our King and Saviour. If we see in the bread and wine that sin leads to the judgment of death, and that Jesus died for sin, but we don't ask Jesus to take that judgment for us, then we are still under judgment.

So what do we need to do before taking the Lord's Supper (v 28)?

We don't need to be sinlessly perfect before taking the Lord's Supper, otherwise Jesus wouldn't have given bread and wine to his sinful disciples (v 23-25)! But we do need to be serious about recognizing where we have sinned; serious about what it cost Jesus to win our forgiveness; and serious about not continuing to live in a way which contradicts the humble unity in our Christ-won salvation that we celebrate at the Lord's Supper.

From the previous study, what actions showed that this church weren't self-examining properly?

⊙ Apply

How, practically, will you make sure you "examine" yourself before you next share the Lord's Supper?

Loving Discipline

Read 1 Corinthians 11 v 30-32

What has happened to some members of the church, and why (v 30)?

What is God's purpose in doing this (v 32)?

It may not seem like it, but God's discipline is good news. There is a consequence of sinning thoughtlessly that is worse than illness, or even physical death: God's "condemnation." Paul wants the Corinthian church to respond to God's discipline by examining themselves, seeing their sin, and coming to the Lord's table in repentance and faith. Not all illness is disciplinary; but these verses teach us to ask whether it might be. It is better for God to allow our lives to be hard now, so that we examine ourselves and come back to trusting Christ instead of wandering away, than for us to have easy lives now, but turn away from Christ and face God's judgment beyond death.

⊙ Pray

Father, thank you for caring about me enough to discipline me when I wander. Please show me ways in which I sin thoughtlessly. As you do this, please thrill me with your Son's love, so I can come to his table more trusting, more humbled, and more thankful. Amen.

~ Notes and Prayers ~

Day
36

Gifts and their Giver

1 Corinthians 12 v 1-11

What are your three top talents? When do you use them, and how?

About Gifts

Read 1 Corinthians 12 v 1

What is Paul's aim in the next section of his letter (v 1)?

If you had to explain the nature and purpose of spiritual gifts to someone right now, how would you do it?

What and Why?

Read 1 Corinthians 12 v 2-7

What does the Holy Spirit enable people to stop doing, and start doing (v 2-3)?

What else does the Spirit do (v 4, 6)?

You can't see the Holy Spirit. But two of the ways the internal work of the Spirit in someone is manifested—shown—is in knowing Jesus as Lord, and in having spiritual gifts.

Why does the Holy Spirit give these "manifestations" (v 7)?

⊙ Apply

How is this different from what the world says about our abilities:

• *in where they come from?*

• *in the reason that we have them?*

Think of the talents you identified at the start. Are there ways you need to change your view of where they're from, and why you have them?

Different Kinds of Gifts

"There are different kinds of gifts," all given by "the same Spirit" (v 4). And Paul goes on to identify some of them.

Read 1 Corinthians 12 v 8-11

This list is not meant to be a complete list of the *charismata*, the gifts of God's grace to us. There are many things the New Testament calls *charismata*, including God's gift of eternal life (Romans 6 v 23) and marriage and singleness (1 Corinthians 7 v 7). We're not meant to get bogged down in exactly what each gift listed here means—I am not sure Paul means absolutely distinct things by each one. The point is that "all these are the work of [the] Spirit," and that he gives them "to each one" (v 11), and so every Christian has a gift to be used "for the common good" (v 7) of the church.

⊙ Apply

Why is it exciting to know that "each one" has been given spiritual gifts?

How are you using yours "for the common good"? Are there ways in which you are using them only for your good?

⊙ Pray

Thank God for your gifts. Ask him to help you spot what they are. Ask him for the humility to lay them at the service of others in your church. Thank him for the opportunities he gives you to do that.

~ Notes and Prayers ~

Your Church Needs You

1 Corinthians 12 v 12-20

If you had to describe what your church is, how would you do so? A (nonphysical) building? A family? A community? All of these are images the Bible uses. But here, Paul uses one of the most famous; that of "the body."

One Body

Read 1 Corinthians 12 v 12-13

What point about the way a body works is Paul making in these verses?

"So it is with Christ" (v 12). Whoever we are—Jews or not, slave or not, rich or poor, old or young—if we have been worked in by the Spirit so that we know Jesus as Lord, we are part of "one body," lived in by "the one Spirit."

This is encouraging! There is no "spiritual elite" in a Christian church. There are no extra levels to be initiated into; no periphery that new Christians need to stay on. If you are a Christian, you are fully part of the body.

This is also challenging. Western society is individualistic. We breathe in the cultural message that our bodies, our talents and our time are all our own, to be put at our own service for our own pleasure. But Paul is saying not only that our gifts belong to the church; our very selves belong to the church, too.

⊙ Apply

Is church there for you, or are you there for your church? How do your actions reflect your answer?

Many Parts

Read 1 Corinthians 12 v 14-20

What mistake could a "foot" or an "ear" make (v 15-16)?

Why does a body need to have parts that are different from each other (v 17)?

Replace "foot" with "new Christian" and "hand" with "pastor"; and "ear" with "shy elderly lady" and "eye" with "confident young evangelist."

What point is Paul making about the church in verses 15-16?

How does Paul explain in verse 19 what he meant by verse 17?

Verse 18 is wonderful. When we look at a local church, God has arranged "the parts"—the people—"every one of them, just as he wanted them to be." God doesn't want you to be someone else, or to have someone else's gifts. He doesn't value one Christian more highly than another. He simply wants you to be you, using the gifts he has given you. We must never make the mistake of the "ear," and think that because we are not someone else, we're not a valuable member of the church.

⊙ Apply

Imagine someone said to you (or you thought about yourself), "I have nothing to contribute to my church." How would verses 14-20 both encourage and challenge you?

~ Notes and Prayers ~

Day
38

You Need
Your Church

1 Corinthians 12 v 21-31

Paul is continuing to picture the church as a body here. He's already said that one part can't look at another part and think, "I'm not really needed." But there's something else each part shouldn't think, either...

Each one Indispensable

Read 1 Corinthians 12 v 21-24a

What shouldn't an eye or a head say to other parts of the body (v 21)?

What does Paul point out about how a body works (v 22)?

A fully-functioning body needs eyes and hands; it requires a head and feet. And so a church member needs all the other church members. No one is dispensable. After all, "God has placed the parts in the body, every one of them, just as he wanted them to be" (v 18).

How would these verses stop some Corinthian Christians feeling proud of their church role, and looking down on others?

⊙ Apply

What kinds of gifts or jobs within church does your congregation tend to think of as "better"? And "less good"?

Are you more likely to think about yourself and your place in church, "They don't really need me" or, "They really, really need me!"?

Each one a Part

Read 1 Corinthians 12 v 24b-31

It seems the Corinthian church had decided that speaking in ecstatic, non-earthly languages—"tongues"—was a special gift, given to special Christians; and that a church full of people speaking in these tongues was a truly Spirit-filled church. But Paul suggests in verse 24b that it is those without obvious gifts or importance who God particularly "honors."

And what does Paul then imply is the real sign of being a Spirit-filled church (v 26)?

Notice that speaking in "different kinds of tongues" is last on the brief list Paul gives of some spiritual gifts (v 28). Paul, under the inspiration of the Holy Spirit, understands the gift of tongues to be something from God, but this is no more special or exalted or spiritual than the gift of healing, or teaching, or guidance. All these—however exciting or otherwise they may seem—are gifts given by the Spirit, for the "common good" of the church (v 7).

Some churches make too much of spiritual gifts; others, too little. But we're about to see that there's something more crucial to have than any spiritual gift—as we'll discover in our next study...

⊙ Apply

How has chapter 12 encouraged and challenged you about:

• *your view of church?*

• *your view and use of your gifts?*

~ Notes and Prayers ~

Day
39

The Most Excellent Way

1 Corinthians 12 v 31 – 13 v 7

This is one of the most famous passages in the Bible. It is often used at weddings—though it is, in fact, a stinging rebuke intended to jolt church members out of being selfish!

Without Love

Read 1 Corinthians 12 v 31 – 13 v 3

The Christian described in these verses is, in a sense, extremely impressive. Here is a believer who speaks in tongues (v 1); who prophesies and has great insights into and knowledge of God's word (v 2); who engages in social action and is prepared to give everything away (v 3). A Christian like this in your church would be amazing!

But without love, what is this Christian (v 2)?

This is the kind of believer the Corinthians wanted to be, and saw themselves as. How would these verses shock them?

⊙ Apply

Honestly, what would you rather be: a respected, gifted, preaching Christian; or an unnoticed, average, loving Christian?

Love is...

Read 1 Corinthians 13 v 4-7

As you read this list, what strikes you as a particularly beautiful aspect of real love?

What would that aspect look like in everyday life?

Think of a falling-out between Christians that you've witnessed, or been part of. What difference would it have made if one or all of those involved had shown this kind of love?

Read 1 John 4 v 7-12

What do these verses tell us about:

- *what love is?*
- *where love is most clearly seen?*
- *how we should respond?*

When God tells us to love others, he is asking us to be like him, and act like him. In his life on earth, and most of all in his death on the cross, God the Son perfectly displayed each of the aspects of love Paul lays out in 1 Corinthians 13.

⊙ Pray

Spend some time thanking God that he is perfectly loving. Pick a couple of descriptions of what love is from 1 Corinthians 13, and thank Jesus for loving you like this.

⊙ Apply

Think of some people who you love (and perhaps those who you struggle to love well). Look through 1 Corinthians 13 v 4-7, and think through how you can love these people with a more Christlike love.

~ Notes and Prayers ~

Day

40

The Greatest of These

1 Corinthians 13 v 7-13

When you think of eternal life in God's presence, what words spring to mind to describe it?

Read 1 Corinthians 13 v 7-13

Never Fails

Western society says that love is a feeling; it ebbs and flows, and sometimes it fails. But God says love is more a decision than an emotion. It is a conscious commitment to do what is best for someone else, no matter how hard, no matter what they do. This is the kind of love that God has for us, and will always have for us. It "never fails."

⊙ Apply

When in your life do you need to remind yourself that your love for someone is not to be based on your emotions, but on your decisions?

"This is love: not that we loved God, but that he loved us" (1 John 4 v 10). How will remembering this change how you love others?

⊙ Pray

Read 1 Corinthians 13 v 4-8a

Substitute your name for the word "love" in Paul's description here.

Which aspects are true of you? Thank God!

Which are least accurate? Pray that God would help you with these aspects of true love.

Never Ceases

What will pass away (v 8)? When (v 10)?

Some people have suggested that by "completeness comes," Paul is referring to the completion of the New Testament; but I think it is far more likely to mean either a Christian entering God's presence when they die, or the day that Christ returns.

On this reading, why is v 12 hugely exciting?

What three things truly matter (v 13)?

"But the greatest of these is love." When we stand in the perfect presence of God, love will remain. When our sight and knowledge of God are perfected, when we see "face to face," we will know and taste and experience pure love.

As the 18th-century pastor Jonathan Edwards put it, "There in heaven, the infinite fountain of love—the eternal Three in One—is set open without any obstacle to hinder access to it, as it flows for ever ... our hearts, as it were, [will be] deluged with love. In every heart in heaven, love dwells and reigns."

⊙ Pray

Thank God for Christians you know who have gone to heaven. Thank him that they are now seeing "face to face," experiencing pure, undiluted love.

Thank God that this is your future. Ask him to make your future change your priorities and perspectives in your present, so you reflect his love today.

~ Notes and Prayers ~

Day

41

Tongues and Prophecies

1 Corinthians 14 v 1-26

I t's important to remember that chapter 13 comes between chapters 12 and 14—it was not written for being read at weddings, but to remind the Corinthian believers that love is more important than gifts, and that gifts used without love are "nothing" (13 v 2).

This is the context in which Paul pens chapter 14...

Read 1 Corinthians 14 v 1-26

A Gift to be Desired

Remember, this church seemed to be exalting speaking in "tongues" above all other spiritual gifts.

So how is verse 1 a correction to them?

What should be their main motivation in seeking gifts (v 12)?

Much ink has been spilled about what "prophecy" actually is! It is unlikely that this was a foretelling of the future. Generally, it seems to have been anything from preaching to simply talking together about gospel truth in conversations—in other words, Spirit-led utterances of biblical truth. We have no reason to think that the Spirit has stopped leading us in this way.

What reasons does Paul give for why prophecy is a greater gift than tongues?

- *v 3-4*
- *v 9*
- *v 18-19*
- *v 23-24*

A Gift for Non-Christians

In verse 21, Paul quotes from Isaiah 28 v 11-12. There, the prophet points forward to a time when God would bring judgment to his rebellious people. The sign that judgment had come would be hearing foreigners talking—because it would show that foreigners had invaded.

So when a non-Christian visits a church, and people speak unintelligibly, it produces (is "for," v 22), unbelievers—people don't understand what is going on, and continue in the life of rejecting God.

But when a non-believer hears the gospel in a way they can understand (i.e. prophecy), they are offered salvation—so prophecy is "for" (i.e. produces) believers.

The Point of Gifts

What's the common message in verses 4, 5 and 17?

This is what Paul is encouraging in verse 12 too, when he talks about using gifts that "build up the church." Paul exhorts the church to pray for, look for and use gifts which will help other believers.

How does the end of verse 26 sum up the section?

⊙ Apply

Are there ways that your church, or you yourself, make too much or too little of certain gifts, as this church did with speaking in tongues?

How are you using your gifts to build up your church? Do you need to be proactive in finding ways to do this?

~ Notes and Prayers ~

Service Order

1 Corinthians 14 v 26-35

Picture what Paul was hearing about the Corinthian church's services. Meetings where many people gave messages in ecstatic tongues at the same time, with few if any being interpreted so others could understand... a number of prophecies—impromptu sermons—of varying lengths, sometimes starting up before the previous one had finished... women shouting out to ask questions or challenge the teaching. It was chaos!

Order, Order!

Read 1 Corinthians 14 v 26-33a

What is the truth about God that Paul reminds the Corinthians of (v 33a)?

This is a part of God's character, shown in the way he always works. He's a God who brought order out of chaos as he created (Genesis 1 v 1-4); he's a God who told a storm to be quiet and still (Mark 4 v 39). And meetings of his people should reflect his character.

Think of some other aspects of God's character—e.g. his holiness, love for the outsider, forgiveness, patience, grace. How can a church's services reveal God by reflecting these qualities?

What should be the guiding principle for what happens in a church service (end of v 26)?

What does this mean practically for the Corinthians (v 26-28)?

Prophecy, too, needs to be ordered so that "everyone may be instructed and encouraged" (v 31). This means that there should not be too many sermons (v 29), and that what is said should be "weighed carefully." Speakers in church meetings are under the authority of the church, which is itself under the authority of apostolic teaching (that is, the New Testament, see verses 36-37). Prophecy isn't to become a field for indulging in selfish competition—it's to be an exercise in Bible-based, selfless encouragement.

Wait till Later

Read 1 Corinthians 14 v 33b-35

These are difficult and controversial verses. Paul's instruction to women to "remain silent" (v 34) seems to be in the context of the public evaluation of prophecies. It is clear from 11 v 5 that Paul expects women to pray and prophesy in church meetings. 14 v 35 suggests that here he is dealing with what women should do when they "want to inquire about something"—stay quiet in the church meeting, and ask "their own husbands" (assuming they are married) afterwards.

⊘ Pray

Thank God for who he is, and pray that your church would reflect this in its meetings. Pray for your own part in doing this.

~ Notes and Prayers ~

Spotting True Maturity

1 Corinthians 14 v 36-40

These verses are the conclusion to Paul's theme in chapters 12 – 14. The Christians in Corinth thought spiritual gifts, especially tongues, equaled spiritual maturity. *Not so,* says Paul.

Real Maturity

Read 1 Corinthians 14 v 36-40

What will a truly mature Christian:

• *remember (v 36)?*
• *acknowledge (v 37)?*

If, on the other hand, they use their gifts in a way which ignores or opposes the "Lord's command," given through the apostles, then they will be (or should be) ignored (v 38).

What else will a truly mature Christian understand?

• *12 v 4-7*
• *12 v 31 – 13 v 3*
• *14 v 1*
• *14 v 32-33*

How does 14 v 39 guard against Christians thinking that speaking in tongues is the mark of a Christian, or of a mature Christian?

How does verse 39 guard against those who want to give no place to speaking in tongues?

What does Paul want to remind the Corinthians of in verse 40?

Paul does not oppose passion in church services. But he does want this passion not to be disorderly.

To Summarize...

1 Corinthians 12 – 14 is one of the most sustained sections of teaching about church in the Bible. It also contains some beautiful, some complicated, and some controversial passages! So it's worth summarizing Paul's main teaching points:

- All gifts come from the Spirit, for building the church (12 v 1-11).

- The church is a body—each part is needed, and each part needs the others (12 v 12-29).

- Without love, gifts are useless (12 v 31 – 13 v 13).

- Prophecy is a gift to be particularly desired, because it builds up believers and makes the gospel clear to nonbelievers (14 v 1-25).

- Church meetings should be varied and passionate, but also orderly, reflecting God's character (14 v 26-34).

⊙ Apply

For each of these points, consider how they make you thrilled to be a church member, and how they challenge you.

⊙ Pray

Spend time thanking God for bringing you into his church, and for your local church body. Thank him for the gifts he's given you. Ask him to show you how you can start, or keep, building up your church with his gifts; and ways he is calling you to grow in maturity, commitment and service.

~ Notes and Prayers ~

_____
_____
_____
_____
_____
_____
_____
_____
_____
_____
_____
_____
_____
_____
_____
_____
_____
_____
_____
_____
_____
_____
_____

Day
44

Taking your Stand

1 Corinthians 15 v 1-11

What do you think life after death will be like?

No one disputes the reality of death; it's what follows it that causes arguments. We now find ourselves in the last main teaching portion of 1 Corinthians; and it's the most extended treatment on the resurrection in the whole Bible.

Hold on!

Read 1 Corinthians 15 v 1-2

What does Paul want to remind these Christians about (v 1)?

Why does it matter so much that they keep "hold[ing] firmly" to it (v 2)?

Paul bookends his teaching on the resurrection with calls to "hold firmly" to its truth (v 2) and to "stand firm" (v 58). But what is the gospel ground from which Christians must never retreat?

Gospel Ground

Read 1 Corinthians 15 v 3-8

The gospel is about a person, all about "Christ" (v 3). God's promised, all-powerful, restoring King is the central subject of the gospel.

What are the essential parts of the message about the Christ?

- *v 3*
- *v 4a*
- *v 4b*
- *v 5-7*

Some people in the Corinthian church were saying "there is no resurrection of the dead" (see v 12). But here, Paul says Christ's resurrection is a core part of the gospel. And he points the Corinthians to two grounds for confidence that it really happened. First, it took place "according to the Scriptures" (v 4)—it was predicted in the Old Testament (e.g. Isaiah 53 v 10-12; Psalm 16 v 10-11). Second, it was witnessed by hundreds of people (v 5-7)—as the Corinthians read this letter, there were at least 251 people (v 6), plus apostles (including Paul, a later addition to the apostolic number, v 8), who were still alive and who had seen the risen Jesus.

Why do even small changes to one of these gospel essentials matter (v 2)?

⊙ Apply

How confident are you that Jesus rose from the dead? How do verses 4-8 increase your confidence?

How would you use these verses to explain the gospel to, and argue for the resurrection with, a non-Christian?

Gospel Grace

Read 1 Corinthians 15 v 9-11

It's this gospel message—of Christ's death in our place, for our sins; his burial; and his resurrection—that changes everything. It transformed Paul from persecutor to preacher (v 9-11). *And it transforms each of us, too!*

⊙ Pray

Re-read verses 3-7, pausing after each phrase to give thanks for each aspect of the gospel that saves you as you hold firmly to it.

~ Notes and Prayers ~

Day
45

If Christ did
not Rise...

1 Corinthians 15 v 12-20

Before you study these verses, ask yourself, *If Jesus hadn't risen from the dead, what difference would that make to my day today?*

The Claim

Read 1 Corinthians 15 v 12-13

What are some of the Christians in Corinth saying (v 12)?

What is the implication of this claim (v 13)?

Do you ever doubt the reality of Christ's historical, physical resurrection from death? What causes you to doubt?

The Consequences

Read 1 Corinthians 15 v 14-19

"If Christ has not been raised..." (v 14)

What are the consequences if Jesus has not risen from the dead?

- *v 14*
- *v 15*
- *v 17*
- *v 18*

So verse 19 is a fair summary of the Christian life if there is no risen Jesus, and therefore no life with him beyond death. "We [i.e. you and me!] are of all people most to be pitied" (v 19). Without the resurrection, Paul's entire life would be pointless. Without the resurrection, the only sensible way to live is to say, as Paul concludes in verse 32, "Let us eat and drink, for tomorrow we die." We might as well get on with enjoying ourselves as best we can now, putting ourselves and our pleasures first—because death mocks all the gifts we have and give.

But Christ has...

Read 1 Corinthians 15 v 20

Why is verse 20 a great relief?!

This is not wishful thinking; it is based on Old Testament prophecy (v 4), and eyewitness evidence (v 5-8). And it changes everything. Paul calls Christ's resurrection "the firstfruits" (v 20). In the Old Testament, this was the first portion of the grain that the Israelites harvested; the part which proved there would be a full harvest to come. Jesus' resurrection is the preview, the first installment, and the beginning of the general resurrection of all who have faith in him. His resurrection guarantees yours.

Work back through v 14-19; turn each of the consequences into its opposite to complete the sentence: Since Christ HAS BEEN raised...

- *v 14*
- *v 15*
- *v 17*
- *v 18*

⊘ Pray

Thank God for raising Jesus, the firstfruits, from the dead. Thank him for all the implications of the resurrection. Ask him to help it make a difference to your feelings and priorities today.

~ Notes and Prayers ~

Our Future in Christ

1 Corinthians 15 v 20-34

Now Paul gives us a short, sweeping history lesson, one which is breathtaking in its grandeur—and one which includes the future.

The Past

Read 1 Corinthians 15 v 20-22

What two things come "through a man" (v 21)?

We are all born "in Adam" (v 22), born into a human race that has been sinful ever since Adam sinned. In this sense, all people belong to, and with, Adam.

And what happens to those who are "in Adam" (v 22)?

What is the alternative (v 22)?

Death came to humanity on a particular historical day, as Adam sinned. Life was offered to humanity on another historical day, as Christ rose. Ultimately, Paul says, we all belong either to Adam, and share his death—or we belong to Christ Jesus, and share his resurrection life.

The Future

Read 1 Corinthians 15 v 23-28

Christ, the "firstfruits" or guarantee, has already risen (v 23).

What will happen in the future (v 23)?

At that point, what else will happen (v 24)?

What a splendid, glorious picture this is!

Christ will destroy all opposition to God—and his people will enjoy his perfect, eternal rule. Christ is reigning now (v 25), from his heavenly throne, but that reign is partially hidden and not yet complete in all its purposes (v 25-27).

But the day is coming when it will be complete, when he will have "put everything under his feet" (v 27). The resurrection guarantees it.

The Present

Read 1 Corinthians 15 v 29-34

We are not sure exactly what Paul is referring to by baptism for the dead (v 29). But his point simply seems to be that the Corinthian church's practice when it comes to baptism is inconsistent with there being no resurrection.

What point does Paul make in verse 33?

If we know that Jesus is risen, and that we will be raised, what impact will that have on our lives now (v 31, 34)?

⊙ Apply

A believer's future is certain and wonderful!

How could you call it to mind more often in your everyday life?

Why is it tempting to live as though verse 32 is ultimate reality?

Do you spend more time with friends who live for today, or with friends who live for their eternal future?

What impact does that have on your view of life?

~ Notes and Prayers ~

Day

47

What Kind of Body?

1 Corinthians 15 v 35-58

When Paul preached in Athens, people "sneered" at the idea of the resurrection of the dead (Acts 17 v 32). Similar sneering questions were being directed at Christians in Corinth (1 Corinthians 15 v 35). In answering them, Paul is going to describe in stunning terms the future that we can look forward to.

Read 1 Corinthians 15 v 35-58

Which verse particularly thrills you?

Imperishable Splendor

Paul uses the illustration of a seed. What point is he making in verses 36-38?

Beyond our resurrection, we will still be us. We will still be human. We will still be physical. But we will be different, too—we will be greater in "splendor."

What is the difference between "the body that is sown" (i.e. our current bodies) and the body that "is raised" (v 42-44)?

"Natural" (v 44) means earthly and sinful, and therefore decaying and dying. "Spiritual" (v 44) is contrasted to this—so it means heavenly, flawless and eternal.

At the Last Trumpet

Whose likeness will we bear in our future eternal lives (v 49)?

Our resurrection life will be just like that of Jesus. And so our bodies, too, will be just like his was after his resurrection—real and physical, and yet also splendid and eternal (see, for instance, Luke 24 v 36-43). In the resurrection appearances of Jesus in the Gospels, we catch just a glimpse of the life we are heading for.

The coming of that eternity will be announced by "the last trumpet" (v 52)—the day of Jesus' return in glory.

What will happen to Christians then (v 51, 53-54)?

The only reason death came to the world, and the only reason to fear death, is because of sin, which means our dying brings judgment and hell. Death stings because of sin (v 56). And sin's power is the law, God's perfect standards which we have failed to meet. But Jesus came to earth, kept the law perfectly, and suffered the sting of death in our place...

... so what can we now say (v 55, 57)?

Our future is guaranteed, physical, perfect.

What three things should we therefore do, says Paul (v 58)?

Why (v 58)?

⊙ Apply

We will be changed—from mortal to immortal, sinful to victorious. However great life is, we know our best days are still ahead of us. However hard life is, we know our best days are ahead of us.

How does this vision of your future encourage you today?

What "work of the Lord" are you motivated to give yourself to more fully today?

~ Notes and Prayers ~

Day
48

Set Aside a Sum

1 Corinthians 16 v 1-4

Paul has written to encourage this church to embrace and display a humble, caring, self-denying love—a Christ-like love. That's the underlying theme of this last chapter, where Paul turns to showing this local church how to relate to God's people further afield.

The Unity of Giving

Read 1 Corinthians 16 v 1-4

What are these verses about (v 1)?

Paul is writing from Ephesus (on the west coast of what is now Turkey) to the church in Corinth, across the Aegean Sea in southern Greece. The "Galatian churches" (v 1) are those he planted in Turkey. As he writes, a great famine is engulfing the people in Jerusalem, hundreds of miles south-east of both Ephesus and Corinth. The "collection" was being made to support the Christians there.

What does Paul say should happen (v 2)?

How should each person's giving be decided?

What will happen after that (v 3)?

These were largely Gentile churches, sending money to the mainly Jewish congregations in Jerusalem.

So, how would this financial giving be a powerful statement about the nature of the world-wide church?

The Gift of Giving

Read 2 Corinthians 8 v 7-19; 9 v 6-11

This is from Paul's second letter to this church; it seems they had been quite slow to obey his words in 1 Corinthians 16!

What does Paul call giving (2 Corinthians 8 v 7)?

That is, giving is an undeserved gift from God—not just to the recipient, but also to the giver. It's a privilege to have enough to be able to give some away to believers we will probably never meet in this life.

How should we decide what to give (9 v 7)?

What should be the attitude of giving (v 7)?

How can we give generously and cheerfully?

Only if we remember that God, not our bank accounts, is where we find what we truly need in life (v 8). How can we be sure of this? Because he has proved it, through coming to earth, giving up the riches of heaven, and dying on a cross to make us eternally wealthy (8 v 9).

⊙ Apply

How do these passages motivate you to give financially to other Christians?

What practical lessons about how to give have you taken from them?

Are there any changes you need to make?

⊙ Pray

Thank Jesus for his grace in giving up so much to make us so rich. Thank Jesus for his grace in giving us resources which we can give up and give away.

~ Notes and Prayers ~

Teachers and Members

1 Corinthians 16 v 5-18

Another aspect of the Corinthians' church life that needs to change is what they look for in a teacher, and what they expect of themselves. Remember that, way back in chapters 2 and 3, we saw the divisions in the church caused by selfishness and leadership rivalry.

Paul's Plans

Read 1 Corinthians 16 v 5-9

What is Paul hoping to do (v 5-7)?

Why is he not heading over to Corinth right now (v 8-9)?

What does this tell us about Paul's own ministry priorities?

And Paul will do this even when "there are many who oppose me" (v 9). Enjoying an easy life was never his priority!

Timothy's Welcome?

Read 1 Corinthians 16 v 10-18

Because he can't come immediately himself, Paul is planning to send Timothy, his young mission partner.

How should he be treated, and why (v 10-11)?

Paul knew the Corinthians would rather have him, an apostle, visiting them, instead of a junior member of his team. And verse 12 suggests they'd perhaps rather have Apollos than Timothy. But what counts is that Timothy is a man who works for the Lord—and this church should welcome him on that basis alone.

⊙ Pray

Do you ever find yourself focusing on what your pastor doesn't do, rather than the gospel teaching that he does do?

Give thanks for the leaders God has given your church. Thank him for their careful teaching of the gospel of Christ. Ask him to encourage them today to keep doing this, using all the gifts he has given them to do it.

Members' Refreshing

Next, Paul looks at the examples of Stephanus, Fortunatus and Achaicus (v 17). These seem to be church members, rather than church leaders.

Why are they a good example (v 15, 18)?

How should such church members be treated (v 16, 18)?

I love the way the King James Version translates verse 15b: "They have addicted themselves to the ministry of the saints." What a wonderful church it would be where every member was besotted with serving and preferring one another, totally committed to inconveniencing themselves to care for one another.

⊙ Apply

Who do you know who is like this? Why not thank them this week?

How can you be more and more this kind of church member? Why not make a specific change this week?

~ Notes and Prayers ~

Day

50

Loving Strength, Strong Love

1 Corinthians 16 v 13-14

In many ways, the verses we're focusing on here are the summary and application of the whole letter.

Them Then

Read 1 Corinthians 16 v 13-14

Verse 13 calls for the development of a military-style self-discipline. But verse 14 shows that this needs to be combined with love.

Think of some of the issues the Corinthian church was struggling with, that we've seen in this letter. How would doing "everything in love" begin to solve those problems?

As Christians, we need to hold verses 13 and 14 together in everything we do. We need all the courage and strength we can get, because the Christian life is hard. But this strength is not one of contracted, constricted, tough, tense coldness. It is expansive, outgoing, kind, caring and warm—because it is a loving strength.

But equally, Christian love is not about adopting some kind of disembodied, disengaged cheerfulness, refusing to deal with the world as it is. Christian love calls us not to desert but to stand guard, not to give up but to stand firm, not to avoid conflict in cowardice but to defend truth in courage.

How has Paul shown this kind of love in the way he has written this letter?

Us Today

"Greater love has no one than this: to lay down one's life for one's friends" (John 15 v 13).

Think of some examples from Jesus' earthly ministry where he displayed the qualities Paul lists in these verses.

⊙ Apply

Which do you find comes more easily to you: strength, or love?

Take each of Paul's commands in these two verses and think about an area of your life where you need to keep, or start, obeying it:

• *Be on your guard*

• *Stand firm in the faith*

• *Be courageous*

• *Be strong*

• *Do everything in love*

⊙ Pray

Thank Jesus for perfectly embodying this kind of loving strength and strong love.

Thank him for the Scriptures, and particularly this letter, which are both strong and loving in content and tone.

Thank him for working in you to produce strength and love in your heart. Speak to him about ways you want to grow in these areas.

~ Notes and Prayers ~

Day
51

And Finally...
Love

1 Corinthians 16 v 19-24

And so we reach the end of this letter—and, as so often throughout it, the key word is "love."

One Another

Read 1 Corinthians 16 v 19-20

This is a family portrait. Aquila and Priscilla, who had once lived in Corinth, greet this church "warmly" (v 19). Paul's co-workers are "brothers and sisters" of theirs (v 20). And church members should greet each other with a "holy kiss," a sign of friendship, because they are all God's children.

What do you think Paul wants to remind the Corinthians of by including these verses?

The Lord

Read 1 Corinthians 16 v 21-23

What is the warning of verse 22?

This is a great reminder that there is no middle ground. We either love Jesus as our Lord, or we will be cursed by him as our Judge. The start and end of the Christian life is loving the Lord Jesus. If we don't, we are simply not part of God's people.

Why did this church need to hear that challenge?

Paul follows this stark warning with a wonderful assurance, in v 23. "Grace" is God's kindness given to us despite us.

Why did this church need to hear that assurance?

⊙ Apply

There are times when we particularly need to be challenged to love Jesus, and to love having him as our Lord—to ask ourselves, "Am I part of his people?"

At other times, we most need to remember the assurance that the Lord Jesus' grace is with us. Through what he has done, we can be part of his people!

Which do you need to remember particularly today? Why?

The Apostle

Read 1 Corinthians 16 v 24

What does Paul assure them of, to finish?

Think of all we've seen of this church's flaws and problems in this letter.

Why is verse 24 a surprising way to end?

Paul could have been angry about the years he had apparently wasted on this church, over the teaching they had ignored, over their selfishness and self-importance. Instead, he loved them. He loved them enough to write. Enough to rebuke. Enough to risk unpopularity. Enough to point them back to Christ.

⊙ Pray

Confess to the Lord Jesus ways in which you have failed to love him. Thank the Lord Jesus for pouring out his undeserved grace to you.

Ask the Lord Jesus to help you to love others as he has loved you, and in the way Paul loved this church.

~ Notes and Prayers ~

Day
52

Being a
Loving Church

1 Corinthians 11 – 16 reflection

First Corinthians is not a short letter, nor is it an easy one. It is seriously exciting, and searingly challenging. And all the way through chapters 11 to 16, Paul is showing us how to be a loving church. So as we finish our time with Paul and this young church in ancient Greece, let's read and reflect on a few key passages from the second half.

For each, in the journaling space provided, write down what most encourages you, and what most challenges you.

Approaching the Lord's Supper

Read 1 Corinthians 11 v 23-32

_____

_____

_____

_____

_____

_____

_____

_____

Using Spiritual Gifts

Read 1 Corinthians 12 v 1-7; 14 v 36-40

_____

_____

_____

_____

_____

_____

Your Place in your Church

Read 1 Corinthians 12 v 12-23a

_____

_____

_____

_____

_____

The Crucial Ingredient

Read 1 Corinthians 12 v 31b – 13 v 7

_____

_____

_____

_____

_____

Where we're Headed

Read 1 Corinthians 15 v 20-28, 50-58

_____

_____

_____

_____

_____

_____

Being Exemplary Members

Read 1 Corinthians 16 v 15-18

_____

_____

_____

_____

_____

_____

_____

⊘ Pray

Thank God for all the ways in which he has excited you and shaped you through this letter. Use you thoughts on the passages above to guide your praise of God and your prayers to him today.

Day
53

I am
With you

Jeremiah 1 v 1-10

For many Christians, the book of Jeremiah is uncharted territory. We know it's in the Old Testament, but we may not know much about what's in it! Digging into the story and preaching of this amazing prophet will not be easy, but it will give us much-needed perspective and reorient our hearts.

The Background

Read Jeremiah 1 v 1-3

Jeremiah was a priest, whose ministry began around 627 BC. At this point, Israel (the northern kingdom of God's people) had been conquered and destroyed by Assyria, and only the southern kingdom of Judah remained (although, confusingly, Jeremiah sometimes refers to "Judah" as "Israel"!) Jeremiah served the LORD from the reign of Josiah, the last faithful king in Judah, until after Jerusalem fell to the Babylonians in 587 BC.

So Jeremiah lived and prophesied during a time of spiritual decay in Judah. Most of his ministry was met with hardheartedness and rejection. At one point Jeremiah would even be thrown into a pit by his enemies!

The Call

Read Jeremiah 1 v 4-10

God is calling Jeremiah to be his prophet.

What is amazing about what God says in verse 5?

Why did Jeremiah feel ill-equipped to be God's mouthpiece (v 6)?

But Jeremiah isn't called to be creative. It's not up to him to decide what to say.

How does God encourage him in these verses? (Hint: look for the word "for.")

Jeremiah's message is not his to change, because it is God's message. We'll see as we go through the book that what he has to say doesn't always make his hearers happy! But it will always be God's words.

What kind of ministry will he have (v 10)?

Take a look at the interaction between Moses and God as you read *Exodus 4 v 10-16.*

Compare Moses' call to ministry with Jeremiah's. What is the same? What is different?

Why do you think the LORD *chooses people like this to do his work?*

⊙ Apply

God does not call those who are equipped. He equips the called.

How does this encourage you in your Christian life today?

Are there any ways in which you need to take the plunge and speak for God as you trust in him to help?

⊙ Pray

Lord, thank you that you use weak, ill-equipped believers like Jeremiah, and like me, to achieve your purposes. Please give me that privilege today. Help me to trust you when I feel too ungifted or unprepared to take risks to serve you. Amen.

~ Notes and Prayers ~

Day

54

Disaster is on its Way...

Jeremiah 1 v 11-19

Jeremiah may have thought that being a prophet in God's service would be a prestigious position. But we're about to see that the message God gives him isn't going to win him any popularity contests in Jerusalem.

An Almond Branch

Read Jeremiah 1 v 11-12

An almond branch (v 11) might not mean much to us, but an Israelite would know that almond trees were the very first to blossom in the spring; in that way they "watched for spring."

What is God doing with his word (v 12)?

God always does what he says he's going to do (see Isaiah 55 v 11).

Why would Jeremiah need to know this before he begins to speak on behalf of God?

Look up these promises that God makes to his people in his word: *Matthew 11 v 28-29; Romans 8 v 37-39; 1 John 1 v 9; Revelation 3 v 5.*

Why is it so exciting to read these words and know that God always watches over his word to fulfill it?

A Boiling Pot

Read Jeremiah 1 v 13-16

What is the next vision (v 13)? What does it mean (v 14-16)?

Just as God promised, this came true in Jeremiah 39 v 1-10. The fact that God keeps his word is bad news for those in rebellion against him!

In 1 v 16, God gives his reasons for bringing judgment on Jerusalem.

What is their crime?

What does God's anger about these things tell us about him?

An Iron Pillar

Read Jeremiah 1 v 17-19

The people of Judah won't go down quietly.

What does God promise Jeremiah (v 19)?

Notice that this isn't a promise of a life free of difficulty; God only promises that his enemies won't destroy Jeremiah!

⊙ Apply

In what ways is verse 12 an encouragement to you today?

Does it need to be a challenge to you in any way?

If you are under pressure for living as a Christian, how can you use verse 19 to help you keep going?

~ Notes and Prayers ~

Day
55

Witness for
the Prosecution

Jeremiah 2 v 1-13

H ere, we meet God acting as a prosecuting attorney, bringing a charge of
faithlessness and idolatry against his people. Try hearing these verses as
though it's a lawyer making his case!

How it used to be...

Read Jeremiah 2 v 1-3

In these words spoken to Jerusalem, the heart of Judah, the LORD reminds them of
their past love and fidelity. In fact, given the way God's people (back then, called "Israel") behaved in the wilderness on their way to the land, complaining and accusing
God (e.g. Exodus 16 v 1-3), he is being gracious in his description of them!

Why is this an important place for the prosecution case to begin, do you think?

Cross-examination Begins

Read Jeremiah 2 v 4-8

How has God treated Judah?

How has Judah treated God?

The LORD is undermining any defense the people of Jerusalem might come up with. He asks them, *How have I wronged you, that you have loved false gods? What excuse can you possibly have?*

Think about what the opposite of each of God's accusations here would look like. How should Israel/Judah have responded to God's kindness towards them?

Broken Cisterns

Read Jeremiah 2 v 9-13

In verse 9, the LORD brings charges against his people. It's the language of an Israelite court of law.

What is the crime (v 8, 11)?

Water from cisterns was not clean. A broken cistern held no water at all.

How does God sum up what has happened (v 13)?

What is the great tragedy of turning away from the true God and worshiping other things, i.e. sinning?

⊙ Apply

Has sin lost its shock value for you?

Have you grown accustomed to it?

Are you behaving in ways that are inconsistent with the love and kindness that God has shown to you?

How have you been looking for "living water" in "broken cisterns"?

What would it mean for you to look to God instead?

⊙ Pray

Lord, forgive me for the ways that I have looked for joy and hope in something other than in you. You have been so kind to me in Christ. Help me to see that sin cannot satisfy, so that I might turn to you for all that I need. Amen.

~ Notes and Prayers ~

Day
56

Serve.
Fault.

Read Jeremiah 2 v 13 – 3 v 5

G od continues to describe what his people have done. To sum it up: they've refused to love him and live under his rule—and they're smug about it!

From Son to Slave

Read Jeremiah 2 v 14-19

The Old Testament calls Israel God's son, his bride, and his prized possession (e.g. Hosea 11 v 1). But now Judah, all that was left of the old unified kingdom of God's people, had become driftwood on the ocean of international politics.

Different nations had taken turns plundering and enslaving its people. The LORD had removed the protection he once afforded to them (Jeremiah 2 v 3).

Why is this happening to Judah (v 17—v 14 confusingly calls Judah "Israel"!)?

Whose fault was it?

How should Judah have responded to this situation, do you think? How did they (v 18)?

You're Going to Serve Somebody

Read Jeremiah 2 v 20-25

The LORD had delivered the nation from cruel slavery in Egypt so that they could serve him as his treasured people.

What did they do instead (v 20)?

Bob Dylan once sang, "You're gonna have to serve somebody." That was true for ancient Israel; they did not want to serve the LORD... but they simply served idols, false gods, instead.

We all serve something, or somebody, as what we think will give us what we need.

Think back to the last time you didn't live as God says. At that point, what were you serving instead of him?

A Discipline Problem

Read Jeremiah 2 v 26 – 3 v 5

What have the people treated as a god (v 27)?

How does God respond to their cry for help (v 27-29)? Why is this perfectly justified?

In response to their idolatry, God has lovingly withheld his good gifts, to try to show them their folly (3 v 3).

How do they respond (v 3-5)? What do they continue to do (end of v 5)?

⊙ Apply

Re-read Jeremiah 2 v 27-28.

What idols are competing for your devotion—for your love, trust or hope? Ask yourself, "What will this be able to do for me in my time of greatest need? What about when I die?"

We need to see our idols for what they ultimately are: helpless and useless!

⊙ Pray

Ask God to help you recognize, and be honest about, where you have worshiped idols.

Then *read 1 John 1 v 9*. We can confess our sins confident of forgiveness!

~ Notes and Prayers ~

Day
57

It's not too Late

Jeremiah 3 v 6 – 4 v 4

This passage is extraordinary. Despite his people's relentless spiritual adultery, the LORD still wants to bless them!

Then and Now

Read Jeremiah 3 v 6-14

Remember that at this point (some time after 627 BC) God's people had split into two nations: the northern one (still called Israel, but which had been destroyed) and the southern kingdom (Judah). The northern was more rebellious than the southern kingdom; but Judah proved to be a fast learner, and eventually surpassed her sister in wickedness!

How is the sin of Israel and Judah described (v 6, 8-9)? How does this help us see why sin is so serious?

Why do you think the people might conclude it was too late to turn back to God now?

What would it look like for the unfaithful people to "return" (v 12-13)?

The people of Judah would have said they had returned to obedient relationship with God!

But what does God know (v 10)?

There's the world of difference between saying sorry to get out of trouble, and saying sorry with heartfelt remorse and desire to change. And God always knows which is which!

Wanted: Circumcised Hearts

Read Jeremiah 3 v 15 – 4 v 4 (if you're pushed for time, read 3 v 19-22, 4 v 3-4)

God makes clear that his desire is to bless his people. There's still time for them to come to their senses and return to him.

Physical circumcision was a sign of being part of God's people, trusting his promises and seeking to obey him.

But what is the "circumcision" that really matters (4 v 4)? What do you think this means?

Go through these verses and pick out the promises that the LORD makes to his people if they will repent of their sin.

Why do you think God insists his people repent before he blesses them? What would happen if he blessed them while they were still pursuing false gods?

⊙ Apply

From this passage, what is real repentance? What is its opposite?

Are there things which you are not really repenting of? How does 3 v 19 encourage you to truly turn back to God right now?

⊘ Pray

Thank God for dealing with your rebellion against him on the cross. Thank him for making you his. Ask him to help you truly repent.

~ Notes and Prayers ~

_____

_____

_____

_____

_____

_____

_____

_____

_____

_____

_____

_____

_____

_____

_____

_____

_____

_____

_____

_____

_____

_____

_____

_____

_____

Beware of
the Lion

Jeremiah 4 v 5-31

These words are not easy for us to hear, just as they weren't easy for the people Jeremiah originally spoke to. But the message is clear: beware of the lion.

Courage will Fail

Read Jeremiah 4 v 5-18

Later in the book, we discover that false prophets were declaring to the people that God would not judge them (see 14 v 13-14). That's what Jeremiah is referring to in 4 v 10. But God's true word, however unpopular, is being spoken through Jeremiah.

What is coming, and what will it do (v 7)?

This is a reference to Babylon, a superpower to the north of Judah.

In what sense is God responsible for this disaster (v 6-8)? In what sense are the people of Jerusalem responsible (v 14, 18)?

PhD in Evil

Read Jeremiah 4 v 19-31

Jeremiah now has a conversation with the LORD. He speaks in verses 19-21, then God responds to him in the rest of the passage. He declares (v 22) that his people are world-class experts in doing evil, but they are morons when it comes to obeying him! Because of their sin, he will destroy their city.

Jeremiah is understandably upset by the LORD's promised judgment.

Does the prophet's response (v 19-21) strike you as disrespectful? Why / why not?

Is it appropriate for God's people to express grief when God sends difficulty?

Verses 23-28 paint a dark picture of what Judah is facing. God is deliberately comparing his judgment with his creation.

How are these verses depicting an "undoing" of God's wonderful creation back in Genesis 1?

God made this world for his people to live in, under his loving rule, knowing the joy of praising him.

Why are verses 23-28 a fitting punishment for how Judah has lived in God's world?

⊘ Pray

Read Luke 21 v 25-28

The world still needs to beware the ultimate Lion, the Son of Man who will return in a cosmic judgment foreshadowed in the devastation Babylon brought to Judah.

Thank God that the Lion is also the Lamb, who died on the cross to take your judgment. Thank him that you can look forward to his coming with anticipation, not anxiety.

~ Notes and Prayers ~

Day
59

Will God
Really Judge?

Jeremiah 5 v 1-31

Rumors were swirling in Jerusalem that the LORD would not really judge people. We hear the same thoughts in some churches today. Sometimes, we hear it in our own heart. Will God really judge?

Should I not Punish?

Read Jeremiah 5 v 1-11

Like Abraham looking for a righteous person in the wicked city of Sodom (Genesis 18 v 23-33, if you've got time to look it up), Jeremiah is sent through Jerusalem to look for a reason why God shouldn't destroy the city. This is really tragic—God's prophet is forlornly searching for anything good in the city of God's people and God's presence.

What does God promise (v 1)?

Where does Jeremiah look, and what does he find (v 3-5)?

Notice God's verdict on them in verse 8. Our society tells us that we realize our humanity most fully when we are free to do whatever we want to do. But the LORD who created us tells us that in fact the absence of self-control, and a culture which exalts feeling as the basis for decisions, makes us like animals.

Think about what Jeremiah sees in Jerusalem. How do you see that in the church today?

How do you think God expects us to answer his question in verse 9?

What will you Do?

Read Jeremiah 5 v 12-31

What do we learn here about:

- *who God is (v 22)?*
- *what the rich in Judah are doing (v 26-28)?*
- *what the spiritual leaders are doing (v 31)?*

It's helpful to think about the kind of people and society God desires, simply by identifying the opposite behavior of what we see in a passage like this!

Do this now, from verses 23-24 and 26-31.

The people "love it this way" (v 31). They love a life of rebelling against God. And they love it when their religious leaders lie to them, telling them judgment will not come, that the LORD will never punish. But lies don't change the truth, and the question at the end of the chapter is devastating: what will you do in the end? What hope will sinners have when God's judgment arrives?

⊘ Apply

God's judgment is inevitable. Remember, he watches over his word to see that it comes true (1 v 12).

In this chapter, how have we seen that God's judgment is fair?

Are you willing, unlike Judah, to hear hard truths from God's word?

Which are the truths you're most tempted to ignore?

⊗ Pray

Thank God for church leaders who risk unpopularity in order to teach hard biblical truth.

~ Notes and Prayers ~

Day
60

Standing at the Crossroads

Jeremiah 6 v 1-30

Again, these verses are not easy to hear. God is using vivid imagery to describe the coming disaster.

Peace or no Peace?

Read Jeremiah 6 v 1-15

What image in these verses particularly strikes you? What is it showing about God's coming judgment?

Why do you think God continues to repeat the charges against the people (v 13-15)?

What message does Jerusalem continue to listen to (v 13-14)? Why is it easier to listen to this than to God's prophet Jeremiah?

Don't miss the damning verdict of verse 10: this is the people of the LORD, who he's rescued from slavery, given a land, blessed with peace and prosperity; and they find his words offensive and close their ears to what he wants to say.

Do we see this in our own day? If we do, how?

Do you ever find yourself doing this?

If you do, what causes it?

Unused Ancient Paths

Read Jeremiah 6 v 16-26

When the Babylonians come, Jerusalem will be terrified. Hemmed in on all sides, the people will be paralyzed and helpless.

Judah is at the crossroads. What path should they take, and why (v 16)?

God has appointed messengers, "watchmen" (v 17), to see the coming judgment and warn God's people.

How do the people respond (v 16-17)?

The people had not completely forsaken the rituals of Old Testament worship. They kept bringing offerings and sacrifices to the LORD (v 20). But without faith, love, and obedience, all of these rituals mean less than nothing!

This is a repeated theme of the prophets. If you have time, read one or both of *Isaiah 1 v 13-17 and Amos 5 v 21-24.*

⊘ Apply

How does this challenge us if we're baptized, churchgoing or communion-taking?

How does this encourage us if we're people who listen to God's words, love his law, and follow his Son?

I have Made you a Tester

Read Jeremiah 6 v 27-30

Jeremiah's prophecies are like the fire and hammer of a silversmith. They could purify the people; but since they won't listen, the "metal" of Judah is rejected.

⊙ Pray

Lord, help me to love you and so walk in your ways today. Enable me to love listening to you, even when your words challenge me and my ways. Amen.

~ Notes and Prayers ~

Day
61

Church Doesn't Save

Jeremiah 7 v 1 – 8 v 3

Jeremiah is given a message for the people coming to the temple. Do you think the good temple-going people are going to enjoy being told to repent?!

The Temple won't Save you!

Read Jeremiah 7 v 1-15

Some people were confident that God would never destroy Jerusalem because the temple was located there. They comforted each other, "This is the temple of the LORD" (v 4). But in verses 12-14 the LORD draws attention to Shiloh, the previous site of his sanctuary. God shut it down because of persistent sin. God is saying, *I've done it before and I will do it again.* Trust in a physical location, in a religious institution, is foolish!

What does the LORD want from the people (v 5-7)? What promise does he make to them if they will do what he wants?

But they won't change (v 8). They go on complacently assuming that they can live as they like, come along to the temple, and God will be satisfied.

Why is that so offensive to God, do you think?

⊙ Apply

What would a person with this attitude look like in your culture and in your time?

Is there any danger of you falling into this trap?

Past the Point of no Return

Read Jeremiah 7 v 16-29

What is shocking about verse 16?

So great is their wickedness and provocation that God has decided he will pour out his wrath on them. There comes a point when it is too late to return.

What is the real sign that someone is part of God's people (v 22-23)?

How would this have been challenging to the temple-goers? How is it a useful reminder for church-goers today?

A Gruesome Scene

Read Jeremiah 7 v 30 – 8 v 3

This description of Judah's wickedness is revolting. They put false gods in the LORD's temple (v 30); they set up altars on which to sacrifice their children (v 31).

How does the coming punishment (8 v 1-2) fit their crimes?

What is God telling us about his character?

God is wrathful because he is holy and sin is terrible. He would not be good if he allowed sin and evil, however well-disguised by religious observance, to flourish— including our own.

⊙ Pray

"While we were still sinners, Christ died for us" (Romans 5 v 8).

Thank God that he deals with sin. Admit yours to him now, and thank him that his Son bore the wrath described in Jeremiah 8 in your place. How humbling! How wonderful! How amazing!

~ Notes and Prayers ~

_____

_____

_____

_____

_____

_____

_____

_____

_____

_____

_____

_____

_____

_____

_____

_____

_____

_____

_____

_____

_____

_____

Day
62

Shameless
and Senseless

Jeremiah 8 v 4 – 9 v 9

The book of Jeremiah is not one long sermon, but a collection of messages given at different places and different times. So while the message might seem repetitious to us, it wasn't for Jeremiah's audience. Anyway, as we've seen, they really, really needed to hear his message! And clearly, since the Holy Spirit has chosen to preserve the repetition for us, we really need to hear this, too.

Knocked off Course

Read Jeremiah 8 v 4-17

If someone falls down, they know well enough to get up. If someone walks away, they usually return. But the LORD declares that his people have abandoned his ways and don't have the sense to return to him.

What is spectacularly foolish about what they're doing in verse 8?

In verse 12, God describes the leaders of the people as lacking shame for their sins. The priests were sacrificing to false gods, the prophets were lying to the people, the scribes were changing God's word. After a while, they lost their capacity to even blush or feel guilty for what they were doing.

Read 1 Timothy 4 v 1-3

The apostle Paul speaks of people whose "consciences have been seared."

What role does your conscience play in keeping you from sin? When do you find it hardest to listen to it?

No Healing

Read Jeremiah 8 v 18 – 9 v 2

This section contains Jeremiah's expression of sadness, a complaint by the people of Jerusalem (8 v 20), and then Jeremiah's (or, possibly, the LORD's) response.

What is Jeremiah saying? What do the people say?

Why has the wound of the people not been healed? Is there really no healing for their injuries? (Hint: look back at 8 v 11.)

Liar, Liar

Read Jeremiah 9 v 3-9

God brings out yet another charge against his people: their mouths are full of lies and malice.

⊘ Apply

What are the "sins of the tongue" you most often struggle with?

What excuses do you find for them?

What needs to change?

⊙ Pray

Remember God watches his word, to see that it is fulfilled (1 v 12).

Thank God that, in a world where words are so often misused, what he says is always true—totally trustworthy. Ask him to help your words today to reflect his.

~ Notes and Prayers ~

Day
63

Death in the Streets

Jeremiah 9 v 10-26

When the justice of God meets the sin of humanity, only the wise will understand what is happening. So then, what does that kind of wisdom look like?

Cue Mourning

Read Jeremiah 9 v 10-22

God's judgment will be extensive and devastating; death will prowl through the city like an assassin, cutting down children in the streets and creeping through windows to kill people in their homes. When God sends his wrath, corpses will lie in the fields like litter.

With that grim picture, we might be tempted to wonder if God is not being a bit harsh. But Jeremiah (v 12) says that a truly wise man will understand why the inevitable disaster is coming, and why it is just.

What explanation does the LORD give for his judgment?

What purpose are the mourning women supposed to serve?

Something to Boast in

Read Jeremiah 9 v 23-24

What is the only thing worth trumpeting?

What does verse 24 remind us about God's character? Why is it wonderful to be reminded of this in the heart of Jeremiah's warning of deserved judgment?

Read 1 Corinthians 1 v 20-25

Where do we see "the wisdom of God"?

How does Paul contrast God's "foolishness" with the best of human wisdom? What can't man's wisdom do (v 21)?

The Wrong Kind of Circumcision

Read Jeremiah 9 v 25-26

Here God speaks of two different kinds of circumcision: that of the flesh only (mere external compliance with God's law) compared with circumcision of the heart (genuine love for and trust in the LORD).

Which is more important: "heart" circumcision or "flesh" circumcision?

To whom does God compare his people, Judah (v 26)?

Why is that shocking?

Read Deuteronomy 10 v 16 and 30 v 6

What does it mean to have a circumcised heart? Who does the "circumcision"?

⊙ Pray

Thank God that he is just—and loves to be kind to those who know him.

Ask him to enable you to bow to him today, and to love him in your heart and with your actions. Tell him how you'll need help to do this.

~ Notes and Prayers ~

Day
64

Why Worship *That?!*

Jeremiah 10 v 1-25

The human heart is very good at worshiping idols. And a passage like this simply says to us, *Why would you do that?*

A god you have to Carry

Read Jeremiah 10 v 1-5

Where do other nations' gods come from?

What can't they do (v 5)? Why are they pretty useless objects of worship and trust?!

If your god needs you to carry it, instead of being able to carry you, it's not worthy of your heart's love and loyalty!

Worshiping a statue you've made yourself seems self-evidently stupid... What do you think the attraction was for the people of Israel?

A God who is Different

Read Jeremiah 10 v 6-10

How does Jeremiah compare false gods and the LORD? What point is he making?

What overall impression do we get of what the God of Israel is like?

Read Jeremiah 10 v 11-25

Jeremiah contrasts the impotent idols of the world with the LORD who shakes the universe just by speaking.

What effect do idols have on the people who worship them?

How is the relationship between God and Israel described?

Jeremiah has been laying out the inevitability of, and justification for, God's judgment of his people. How is verse 16 a verse of hope?

⊙ Apply

"Dear children, keep yourselves from idols" (1 John 5 v 21).

We may not literally bow down to small blocks of painted wood, but we're still tempted by idolatry. We worship things we've made—money, cars, houses. We love more than God things that will perish and cannot help beyond death—marriage, career, sex, success.

What earthly things do you rely on to give your life meaning and hope?

What things can you not imagine being able to live happily without?

Pick out the three idols you most struggle not to rely on... and then read Jeremiah 10 v 1-16 again with these things in mind.

⊙ Pray

The best way to kill off our idols is to remind ourselves how wonderful the true God is. Spend some time now praising the LORD for who he is.

~ Notes and Prayers ~

_____

_____

_____

_____

_____

_____

_____

_____

_____

_____

_____

_____

_____

_____

_____

_____

_____

_____

_____

_____

_____

_____

_____

_____

_____

_____

_____

Day
65

A Prophet
and a Target

Jeremiah 11 v 1 – 12 v 17

J esus knew that no prophet is welcomed and honored in his own hometown
(Luke 4 v 24). Here, we find Jeremiah discovering the truth of that.

As Many gods as Towns

Read Jeremiah 11 v 1-17

What does God tell Jeremiah to do (v 6-8)?

Why is God brining disaster on those Jeremiah is to preach to (v 9-13)?

Welcome Home?!

Read Jeremiah 11 v 18-23

Anathoth is Jeremiah's hometown (1 v 1).

What do the people there want him to do (v 21)?

How does Jeremiah find out about the plot against him (v 18)? What does he do as a result (v 20)?

How does the LORD respond (v 22-23)? Does he tell Jeremiah to soften his message?

O Lord, Why?

Read Jeremiah 12 v 1-13

Jeremiah pours out his heart to the Lord.

What does he know about God (v 1)? But what is his problem?

Have you ever felt like this? Have you ever known that God is good and just, but also found yourself wondering what he is up to in your life and this world?

The Lord responds by telling Jeremiah that things will get even worse for him (v 5-6)—but that he will ultimately send his vengeance against his people (v 7-13).

Look at 1 v 17-19. What promise had God given Jeremiah for just these circumstances?

⊘ Pray

There's a balance that Christians must maintain. On one hand, we are encouraged to bring all of our fears, doubts, and anxieties to the Lord in prayer. On the other hand, we must bring our feelings in line with the truth about God and his salvation. We need to remember that at the cross, God has shown us both his resolve to judge sin and his love and mercy for his people.

There are times when we need to pour out our hearts and be honest with ourselves and God about how we're feeling. There are other times when we need to listen to ourselves less and preach to ourselves more! If you are downcast today, *read Psalm 42* and make it your prayer... and preach it to yourself, too!

But After...

Read Jeremiah 12 v 14-17

Remember what we've seen about God's people, both in this passage and in the whole book of Jeremiah so far.

What is surprising, and wonderful, about verses 15-16?

What does it tell us about God?

⊘ Pray

Thank God for his justice—that wrongs will be righted. Thank God for his compassion—that his people have been judged at the cross and are forgiven for eternal life.

~ Notes and Prayers ~

Day
66

Picture
This

Jeremiah 13 v 1-27

G od often makes his point through his prophets by using visual aids. And that's exactly what he is doing in these verses.

Your Love is Like...

Read Jeremiah 13 v 1-11

A "linen belt" (v 1) was the seventh-century BC's equivalent of underpants.

What does Jeremiah have to do with his belt (v 1-7)? How does it end up?

What point is this visual aid making (v 8-9)?

How does God sum up what it is that has made Judah like this (v 10)?

In verse 11 God uses the loincloth image in a different way, this time expressing what his hopes had been for the people of Jerusalem.

What is he saying there?

All's Well that Ends... Smashed

Read Jeremiah 13 v 12-14

God uses a popular saying to spring a word of judgment on the people. The saying, "Every wineskin should be filled with wine" was like our, "It will all work out in the end." Here the LORD promises that they will be filled with wine, but it will be much too much for them to handle.

Who will be affected by this "drunkenness"?

What will be the result?

A Leopard's Spots

Read Jeremiah 13 v 15-27

The prophet warns the people that they are like people in the mountains at twilight (v 16). Devastating darkness is coming soon!

How possible is it for these people to "do good" and avoid God's judgment (v 23)?

This passage leaves us with some heavy questions. How can a leopard's spots be changed? How can imperfect people—people like us—become good?

Read these three passages and put together the Bible's answer:

- *Jeremiah 31 v 31-34*
- *John 3 v 1-6*
- *2 Corinthians 5 v 17*

⊘ Pray

Lord, thank you for making me a new creation in Christ. Thank you that you have changed me in ways I could never have done myself.

Thank you that you have made me useful for you. Help me to bring you renown, praise and honor in how I live today. Amen.

~ Notes and Prayers ~

Day
67

The Only Hope is the Hope we Have

Jeremiah 14 v 1 – 15 v 14

I n chapter 14, drought and invasion has come to Judah. God's judgment, warned of repeatedly by Jeremiah, is beginning.

False Promises

Read Jeremiah 14 v 1-10 and 13-22

What does Jeremiah ask God to do (v 7, 9)?

Why does he think God should do something?

How does God answer (v 10)? Why isn't he acting to help his people?

Jeremiah seems to accept this explanation, but he counters with another objection: what about all the other prophets who have been running around saying that the LORD had told them he wouldn't judge the people?

How does God respond in verses 14-16?

Futile Prayer

Read Jeremiah 14 v 11-12 and 15 v 1-14

The LORD patiently listens to Jeremiah's complaints and questions. But he wants to make it clear: Jeremiah's prayers will not help. Even Moses and Samuel, two men famous in the Old Testament for their effective prayers, wouldn't be able to help the situation! It's important to note that the LORD is not saying that he would reject his people if they were to return to him. He is simply saying that Jeremiah's righteous prayers won't be enough to help them, to intercede for them, because of their sin.

Firm Hope

Read Hebrews 7 v 24-25

What is Jesus able to do (v 25)?

What Jeremiah, Moses and Samuel couldn't achieve for sinful people— successfully asking God to save them— Jesus can.

Read Romans 8 v 34

What does this verse remind us that Jesus, who speaks to God on our behalf, has done?

Jesus alone can point to his sin-bearing death and say, *I have taken the judgment she, or he, deserves.* He alone can point to the empty tomb and say, *I have risen from the dead to speak for my people.* Jesus prays for his people, interceding for us, telling his Father that we are his, saved by him to live with him. His prayers are what we need, and what we have!

⊘ Pray

Thank your Father that he has seated his Son and your Savior at his right hand, to intercede for you.

Thank God that Jesus has taken the anger you deserve and given you the life he deserves.

Thank God that, through Jesus, he hears your prayers and acts to help you. Bring your needs and concerns to him now.

~ Notes and Prayers ~

Day
68

Not the End
of the Story

Jeremiah 15 v 15 – 16 v 21

G od's judgment had not yet fallen on Judah. But it had fallen on the northern
kingdom of Israel a hundred years earlier, as the people were taken into
captivity in Assyria, to the north. It looked like the end... but it wasn't.

A New Exodus

Read Jeremiah 15 v 15 – 16 v 15

What does God promise to do for the people of Israel (16 v 15)?

In the Old Testament, when the LORD wanted to show his people that he was the
God who saves, he would remind them that he had delivered them from Egypt (e.g.
Psalm 81 v 8-10). But in Jeremiah 16 v 15, we discover that what God is soon going to
do for Israel will be such an amazing act that it will surpass the exodus out of Egypt.
And about a century after Jeremiah received this prophecy, God kept his promise
and brought his people back to their land.

*Why did God send his people into exile if he was just going to bring them back?! What do
you think they learned through the experience?*

In the Old Testament, God's salvation of his people included delivering them from
a powerful enemy nation.

Read Luke 11 v 14-22. How is our salvation in Jesus similar?

Every Step you Take

Read Jeremiah 16 v 16-18

Even when his people are in a foreign land, the LORD always sees them. They never have an unobserved moment!

What does the LORD see when he looks at these people (v 17)?

What must happen before the LORD restores Israel from exile (v 18)?

⊙ Apply

How does remembering God's omniscience (his complete knowledge of all things) encourage you to avoid sin in your life?

Weak Idols or Powerful LORD?

Read Jeremiah 16 v 19-21

Earlier, Jeremiah had lost his confidence in the LORD and begun to complain bitterly about him (15 v 10-18). In response, God commanded him to repent (15 v 19-21). Now, the prophet responds.

How does he express reliance on God (v 19)?

What will the people learn about the LORD from their exile and return (v 21)?

Israel had put their trust in worthless, weak idols. Now the LORD would bring them back, showing them who was really powerful enough to save them. Surely then they would realize and remember the foolishness of worshiping anything other than the true God!

⊙ Pray

Ask the LORD for grace to see how you are worshiping idols and to see how foolish your worship is. Thank the LORD that he is the true God, and has proved his existence, power and goodness supremely at the cross and the empty tomb. Then ask him to help you to love and worship him at those moments when you are most in danger of loving and worshiping a powerless idol.

~ Notes and Prayers ~

A Horticultural Lesson

Jeremiah 17 v 1-8

I magine walking through a barren desert. Mile after mile, the only plants you see are shriveled, wizened shrubs beaten down by the heat and wind. Then suddenly you see a lush tree loaded with fruit, thriving despite the brutal environment. What has enabled that tree to be different? How does it survive, and thrive?

The Parched Shrub

Read Jeremiah 17 v 1-6

Humans are either that wizened shrub or the healthy tree.

If I trust in, and depend on, myself, what else am I doing (v 5)?

These verses go right against the grain of our culture. We like someone who is independent, a self-starter. We admire the man who is the master of his fate and captain of his soul (as a poet once put it). But the LORD describes this way of living as "cursed."

Where does living like this lead (v 6)?

Read 2 v 13-18. How were the people of Judah trusting in man instead of God?

The Tree by the River

Read Jeremiah 17 v 7-8

A tree in the desert needs access to water or else it will die. The person who trusts in the LORD finds that their roots are established in a spring of life-giving water. They are able to thrive and endure despite the withering blasts that life sends their way.

Look at the picture in verse 8. What does it show about what it means to "trust in the LORD"?

The only man we've seen in this book who lives like this is Jeremiah himself. Which is a great reminder that a blessed life is not the same as an easy life.

How had Jeremiah's life shown the truth of these verses?

Read Psalm 1

What are the similarities between this psalm and Jeremiah 17 v 5-8?

What does Psalm 1 add about how to be blessed?

We're not sure exactly when Psalm 1 was written, but presumably it was at a different time and different place to Jeremiah 17. The message of these verses is universal; it applies in every situation!

⊙ Apply

Our world offers us a lot of different things in which to place our ultimate trust (medicine, technology, government, psychology, family etc.)

What things tempt you to trust them rather than God? What fruit has that borne in your life?

In what areas of your life do you need to trust God fully? What would it look like to grow and thrive and bear fruit in those areas?

~ Notes and Prayers ~

Day

70

The Heart of the Problem

Jeremiah 17 v 9-27

What causes people to do bad things? Is it their upbringing, their education, their relationships? Well, all of those things factor into who we are and what we do. But the Bible locates the source of our trouble inside of us, not outside of us!

Heart of Darkness

Read Jeremiah 17 v 9

Where is our deepest problem located? How is this place described?

Woody Allen once tried to justify a scandalous relationship with a young woman by saying, "The heart wants what it wants." Those words are full of biblical truth!

Ever since Adam and Eve sinned, every aspect of our lives is marred by sin. Our hearts, the center of our emotions and intellect and will, are deceitful and self-protective. We can't trust them or understand them; and even worse, we can't see how deceived we are!

God is helping us to see we can't always trust our hearts to lead us truthfully. *Read Proverbs 12 v 15; 13 v 10; 17 v 10.*

How does the wisdom of those Proverbs help us to live rightly, despite our tendency to self-deceive?

⊙ Apply

What might heart deception look like in your life? Think about:

- *Have you ever justified yourself when you knew you were wrong?*
- *Have you ever been sure that you were right, only to find out that you were totally wrong?*
- *Have you ever found yourself doing something without knowing why you were doing it?*

The Cardiologist will See you Now

Read Jeremiah 17 v 10-27

How does verse 10 answer the question at the end of verse 9?

What does this verse tell us that God will do with this knowledge of us?

This should worry us! A deceitful heart is not going to produce deeds that deserve reward. And such a heart will stop us being able to recognize this!

Read Ezekiel 36 v 25-27

What is the only hope for us?

Read Acts 2 v 38

What is the way to have God work in us like this?

⊙ Pray

Father, thank you for the new heart your Son died to offer me, and your Spirit came to give me. Thank you that I can now see life as it really is, in the light of your word. Show me how to live in line with my Spirit-given heart today. Amen.

~ Notes and Prayers ~

A Potter
and his Clay

Jeremiah 18 v 1-23

Next, Jeremiah takes a trip to a pottery studio. He's not there for a divinely-inspired art and craft project, but for another visual illustration of the truth about God's world and God's people.

Molded by the Potter

Read Jeremiah 18 v 1-11

What does the potter do (v 3-4)?

The clay has no say in any of this!

What point is God making to Israel (v 5-6)?

What is he saying about how far his sovereignty extends?

How does the divine potter work with his clay (v 7-10)?

The God of the Bible doesn't always conform to our sensibilities and preferences (which, by the way, is our problem—not his!). In Jeremiah 18, God asserts that he will do whatever he wants to do, to whoever he wants to do it, whenever he wants it done.

Who is in control of our life and our fate—God or us?

In what ways does this unsettle you, or encourage you, or both?

Water that Doesn't Flow

Read Jeremiah 18 v 12-18

How do God's people respond to the divine potter (v 15)?

How do they respond to his messenger (v 18)?

These were crimes against the order of things, like a mountain river running dry or snow melting at high altitude (v 14).

⊘ Apply

Read Ephesians 2 v 4-10

What has the sovereign God:

• *done for his people (v 5-6)?*

• *given his people (v 8)?*

• *prepared for his people (v 10)?*

How does the reality of God's sovereignty impact the way you think about:

• *prayer?*

• *yourself?*

• *sharing your faith with your friends (remember Jeremiah 18 v 7-8)?*

Rebellious, yet Re-molded

So here we have it—the people of Israel are refusing to listen to the God who made them, rescued them and loves them, and instead plotting to kill his messenger. It's a challenging, unsettling book! We can't rely on our church attendance or religious performance to save us (7 v 4), and we mustn't be deceived either by false teachers who deny that God judges (14 v 14-15) or our own hearts (17 v 9). But wonderfully, we can rely on God, and his compassion—on the God who is always ready to forgive those who hear his warning and turn back to him (18 v 7-8).

Let's praise the Potter, who doesn't destroy rebellious clay, but remakes it— remakes us—new!

~ Notes and Prayers ~

A Smashed Pot

Jeremiah 19 v 1-15

The image of the potter and his clay in the previous chapter is crucial to the book of Jeremiah. The first seventeen chapters have been a warning: a promise from the LORD that terrible judgment will fall on the people of Judah. It will be no help that they belong to God's ancient people—their rebellion will be punished.

But in the potter's studio (chapter 18), Jeremiah has been told that God is free to change his mind if the people repent. God is like a potter, able to start over and re-make a project after it is already underway. In the same way, God will forgive Judah and remake them if they will repent. After all, if that weren't true, then why would the LORD keep sending Jeremiah to warn the people?! If God weren't willing to forgive, he could have just destroyed them a long time ago and saved a lot of ink!

Why is it good news for our world that God is this kind of "potter"?

Why is it a challenging reality?

Hardened Clay

Read Jeremiah 19 v 1-13

The image is a powerful one: you can reshape clay when it's wet, but if a defective piece is dried, it's useless. It can only be smashed and thrown away.

What is the LORD saying about Jerusalem's spiritual state?

What had the people of Jerusalem done to earn this kind of rebuke (v 4-5, 13)?

There are two ways of understanding the message of the broken pot. It could be that the LORD is saying that he'll no longer accept any repentance from his people. On the other hand, it could be that the LORD is simply saying that the hardness of their hearts is such that they will never repent, and thus there is no hope of forgiveness.

Stiff Necks and Closed Ears

Read Jeremiah 19 v 14-15

Another theme of the book of Jeremiah is God's coming judgment of the religious establishment. Here, Jeremiah is in the temple, the place where God's people could make sacrifices so they could enjoy relationship with, and blessing from, God.

But what did they now find the God of the temple giving them? Why?

Re-read verses 4-5. How does this help us see what it means to be "stiff-necked" (v 15)?

⊘ Apply

In what ways do you act in a "stiff-necked" way? What would it look like if you were bowing your head to God as your King instead?

What needs to change? How does the image of the divine Potter with his clay motivate you to change?

⊙ Pray

Ask God to forgive you for times you don't bow to him. Ask him to show you when you are about to be stiff-necked today, and to give you grace to live his way.

~ Notes and Prayers ~

_____

_____

_____

_____

_____

_____

_____

_____

_____

_____

_____

_____

_____

_____

_____

_____

_____

_____

_____

_____

_____

_____

_____

_____

Day

73

Comfort-Seekers Need Not Apply

Jeremiah 20 v 1-18

Does following God mean that your life will be fun and trouble-free? Not if Jeremiah's life is any indication!

Prophet in the Stocks

Read Jeremiah 20 v 1-6

How does Pashhur's job make his treatment of God's prophet even more inexcusable?

Never mind whether or not Jeremiah was speaking the truth—Pashhur thought it was a crime just to suggest that bad things would happen to the city! But Jeremiah would be proved correct.

How would your non-Christian friends respond if you told them about the Bible's message, that God will punish them for their sins?

What makes something true: what God says about it, or how we feel about it? When do you find it easy to forget this?

Dark Night of the Soul

Read Jeremiah 20 v 7-18

In these verses we see Jeremiah's prayers and cries to the LORD.

Does anything he says surprise you? What?

What kinds of mistreatment was Jeremiah experiencing at the hands of his countrymen?

Why doesn't he just stop preaching and prophesying (v 9-12)?

Does God take away the cause of Jeremiah's suffering? What does God do for him?

What do you think of Jeremiah's complaints to God? Is he justified?

Jeremiah is clearly feeling terrible.

What does he teach followers of God to hang on to when they are depressed (v 11-13)?

⊙ Pray

Pray for any Christians you know who are suffering with depression (perhaps your-self). Ask God to help them remember the truths of verses 11-13 as they battle with the feelings of verses 14-18.

The Darkest Day

Jeremiah was persecuted by a powerful priest, taken into custody and publicly mocked, abandoned by friends and left feeling abandoned by God. In those ways, his sufferings point us towards the way the Lord Jesus suffered for us.

Read Hebrews 2 v 17-18

How do the life and experiences of Jesus encourage us to go to him for help when we're struggling with depression or sadness?

If you are in a dark place, it does not mean you are not a Christian, or that God doesn't love you. If you haven't done so already, speak to a trusted Christian friend or pastor, so that they can pray for and help you.

From the next study, we will be picking up the speed with which we are working through the book of Jeremiah, and won't cover every verse. If you have time, use the verses in brack-ets to read the whole book.

~ Notes and Prayers ~

Day
74

Confrontation with the Truth

Jeremiah 21 v 1-10, 22 v 8-9 (21 v 1 – 22 v 30)

Time has passed—and now destruction is looming outside the city walls. A desperate King Zedekiah sends a delegation to Jeremiah to see if the LORD will help.

A Shot in the Dark

Read Jeremiah 21 v 1-10

King Zedekiah was not a righteous man (2 Kings 24 v 18-19). But here, as the king of Babylon besieges the city, he reaches out to the LORD for help.

Who is in this delegation (Jeremiah 21 v 1)? Why does this not bode well (20 v 1-2)?

Given what you know about the book of Jeremiah so far, would you expect that God would turn back the Babylonian invaders because Zedekiah has asked? Why / why not?

How does God answer him (21 v 4-7)? What options do the people of Jerusalem have (v 8-9)?

Read Deuteronomy 3 v 22

Here, the LORD is making a promise to Israel as they prepare to capture the land of Canaan (part of which would become Judah).

What was the promise that the LORD made? Why would that have been important to Israel as a small nation?

Now compare that promise to the LORD's response in Jeremiah 21 v 5.

What is the significance of what he says there?

Why has He Done such a Thing?

Read Jeremiah 22 v 8-9

The LORD offers Jeremiah a script for responding to those who want to understand Jerusalem's destruction.

What specific reasons does he give?

Read Leviticus 26 v 3-8, 14-19

What's the promise and the warning?

How do the events of Jeremiah 21 mirror the punishments God warns about here in Leviticus?

How does that help us make sense of what God says in Jeremiah 22 v 9?

Judah was guilty of breaking God's law, though they refused to accept it; they deserved the punishment of God, though they were unwilling to confront that. We too are law-breakers and deserve God's wrath (Romans 3 v 9-18, 23). But Jesus obeyed God's law perfectly for us. And when we become followers of Christ, God gives us Jesus' righteousness as a gift. We are counted as law-keepers in God's sight.

⊙ Apply

How does this enable you to go to God for forgiveness when you sin?

How does the love God has shown you in the life and death of his Son motivate you to obey him? What difference is this going to make to your day today?

~ Notes and Prayers ~

A Righteous Branch

Jeremiah 23 v 1-6 (23 v 1-20)

When a nation has lost its way, is there any hope? When God's people themselves have lost their way, is there any hope? Yes!

Needed: A New Shepherd

Today, we think of kings as mostly political figures. But ancient Israel was a special kind of nation—a nation of God's people.

And a special nation needed a special kind of king. The kings of Israel were supposed to be shepherds; spiritual leaders who would exemplify, encourage and justly enforce obedience to God's law and rule. The spiritual health of God's people is, in a sense, determined by their leaders.

Read Jeremiah 23 v 1-4

Why is the LORD angry with the "shepherds"?

How will the he treat them (v 2)?

How will the LORD treat his people (v 3)?

Read Genesis 1 v 28. What is the significance of the promise in that they'll one day again "be fruitful and increase in number" (Jeremiah 23 v 3)?

Today, God's people are not a political nation, and so the leaders of God's people are no longer political kings.

Read 1 Peter 5 v 1-4

Who exercises oversight (humanly speaking) over the church now?

What should that oversight look like? How do Peter's instructions remind you of God's promise in Jeremiah 23 v 4?

Who is the Chief Shepherd? What does that tell us about authority in the church?

Promised: A New King

One king who had shepherded God's people properly was David. And God had promised David that one of his descendants would rule over God's people forever (2 Samuel 7 v 11b-16). In Jeremiah's day, that promise seemed to hang by a thread as Babylon carried Judah's king off into captivity. Those who had stayed faithful to God must have wondered whether he had forgotten his promise.

Read Jeremiah 23 v 5-6

What kind of king is God still promising to "raise up"? What will this king do?

What will be the result of this king's leadership (v 6)?

How is this promise ultimately fulfilled? (Hint: read Luke 1 v 32 and 19 v 38.)

⊙ Apply

Even when things look bleak, God is faithful to his promises.

How does that encourage you today?

How does that help you not to worry about tomorrow?

If you live in a nation which has rejected God (or is in the process of rejecting God)... or if your institutional church seems to have turned its back on the real God... how do these verses give you hope? How do they help you know what to prioritize in your prayers?

~ Notes and Prayers ~

Day
76

The Hammer
of God's Word

Jeremiah 23 v 21-30 (23 v 21 – 24 v 10)

A lot of people claim to speak on behalf of God, but their messages sometimes contradict each other. How can you tell the real messenger of God from the phonies and frauds?

Take a moment to actually answer that question! How can you tell the real from the fake?

The Dreams of Liars

False prophets had opposed Jeremiah throughout his ministry. Whenever Jeremiah declared judgment on Jerusalem, his opponents would assure the people that they were safe (e.g. 6 v 13-15). When Jeremiah spoke of God's displeasure with sin, the false prophets would tell them not to worry. And their words sounded more positive and comfortable!

But there's one crucial difference between their words, and Jeremiah's...

Read Jeremiah 23 v 21-27

What authority did the false prophets claim for their message (v 25)? Where did their prophecies really come from (v 26)?

If the false prophets had really listened to God, what would have been the result (v 21-22)?

What was the actual result of their teachings (v 27)?

Why do you think God warns them that he:

• *is the God of the whole world (v 23)?*
• *sees everything (v 24)?*

⊙ Apply

God is no less present everywhere today than he was then.

How does this serve to warn us against indulging the sin in our lives?

Is there anything specific you need to deal with today?

Though it may be intimidating to think that God sees and knows all of our sin, remember that God knew you perfectly and still sent his Son to die for you! Jesus didn't give his life for some better version of you; he knew your sin and still loved you enough to save you.

Straw v Wheat

Read Jeremiah 23 v 28-30

The words of the false prophets are like useless straw, piled up as they quote each other (v 30). But God's word (through Jeremiah) is like wheat that gives nourishment and life (v 28).

To what does God compare his word (v 29)?

What does that tell us about God's word?

Read Hebrews 4 v 12-13

What similarities are there between this and Jeremiah 23? How does this encourage you to spend time reading and hearing God's word? How can you tell the real Christian preacher from the fake?

⊙ Pray

Thank God for those you know who are Christian preachers because they are preaching the Christian gospel, based on Christ's word. And pray for those you know who are suffering under preaching that is "fake"—for discernment to see this, for wisdom to know how to respond, and for humility for you to seek to gently show them the danger they are in.

~ Notes and Prayers ~

The Cup of God's Anger

Jeremiah 25 v 15-29 (Jeremiah 25 v 1 – 26 v 24)

W̶hat happens when a holy, all-powerful God gives judgment to human beings? Again, Jeremiah uses a picture to show us.

The Nations will Drink

If you wanted to kill someone in the ancient world, poisoning their drink was a good way (it's why kings had cupbearers, to test their wine). Old Testament prophets often used the image of a cup to describe God's anger against sin. They spoke of a cup full of God's wrath: bitter, disorienting, and fatal to the drinker.

Read Jeremiah 25 v 15-29

What does the LORD tell Jeremiah to do with "the cup"? Who must he take it to, and what must they do with it?

The LORD's wrath came to the nations through the sword of the king of Babylon (v 27). In fact, his armies eventually destroyed all the nations listed in verses 18-25.

Which nation will be the last one to drink from the cup (v 26—the footnote is helpful)?

Why is that significant?

How should God's willingness to discipline his own people make the nations of the world feel (v 29)?

What do these verses tell us about God? And about humanity?

Passages like these can sometime make us uncomfortable. It can be hard to read about God's intention to destroy entire nations of people.

This passage doesn't tell us why judgment is falling on these nations. But from what you've read in Jeremiah, why do you think God's judgment is coming?

God's wrath is a controversial subject. But think about how you respond when someone you love has been hurt, or when you became aware of some act of abuse and injustice in the world.

Do you ever become angry at those kinds of things? Do you long for justice to come to those who commit these acts?

The cup of God's wrath shows us he is a good, loving God. The opposite of love is not righteous anger: it is indifference. God's wrath is good news as we suffer, but it is terrifying news for us as sinners.

The King has Drunk

Read Mark 14 v 32-42

As God's Son Jesus prayed on the night before his death, he asked his Father to "take this cup from me" (v 36). It seems that he began to experience a foretaste of the wrath of the Father that he would take for his people on the cross.

How does your understanding of "the cup" in Jeremiah 25 help you to begin to appreciate what Jesus did for us on the cross?

⊘ Pray

Thank God that he cares enough about sin to be angry about it. Thank him that he loves you enough to take his wrath upon himself.

~ Notes and Prayers ~

Day
78

God has the Final Say

Jeremiah 27 v 1-11 (27 v 1 – 28 v 17)

S ometimes it can be hard for us to trust that God's will is the best thing for our lives. Here, the LORD calls Jerusalem to do something they that would have been the last thing they would have wanted to do: to submit to a foreign nation.

The Outstretched Arm

The year was 597 BC, and the shifty King Zedekiah of Judah was plotting to get out of his obligation to pay tribute money to Nebuchadnezzar, the king of Babylon. As Zedekiah met with envoys from other nations to scheme together, the LORD sent Jeremiah with a message for the ambassadors to take back to their kings: submit to Babylon's rule or be destroyed.

Read Jeremiah 27 v 1-11

What was the symbolic act that Jeremiah was to perform before the king (v 2)?

Why do you think the LORD had him act out his message as well as speak it?

How do you think the recipients of the message would respond to it?

In verse 5, God makes a significant statement. He alone created the earth and everything in it; that fact is the basis of his authority. As such, he has the ultimate say over everything that happens; he can give power and authority to whoever seems right to him. Who can dare to oppose God's designs?

But just as the LORD gave Nebuchadnezzar power, in the same way he appointed an end to the Babylonian Empire within a few generations (v 7).

What does the LORD offer the kings of the nations as an incentive for obedience (v 11)?

What will be the consequences for disobedience (v 8, 10)?

The Hard Questions

These verses give us some hard questions to ponder. It is important to wrestle with them, but we mustn't worry that we cannot fully answer them...

The Babylonian army was idolatrous, ruthless and bloodthirsty. How could the LORD use them as an instrument for his purposes?

In Jeremiah 50 – 51, we will see God condemning Babylon for destroying Jerusalem. But here, it seems that the LORD intends for them to do that very thing. How might we reconcile those two ideas?

⊙ Apply

Do you believe that God has the authority to tell you what to do? Do your actions prove your answer is really true?!

Is there anything the Lord is calling you to do that you find difficult? How does this passage encourage you to get on with obeying him?

⊙ Pray

Take time to confess your sins and praise the Lord for his creative power, authority, and wisdom. Ask for him to help you remember that you are not him, and that while he knows all things and plans all things, you do not.

~ Notes and Prayers ~

_____

_____

_____

_____

_____

_____

_____

_____

_____

_____

_____

_____

_____

_____

_____

_____

_____

_____

_____

_____

_____

_____

_____

_____

Instructions for Life in Exile

Jeremiah 29 v 1-14 (29 v 1-32)

How do you live when everything has gone wrong in your life? Can you find joy when things aren't going the way you thought they would go?

God's People in Babylon

Read Jeremiah 29 v 1-9

In 597 BC, King Nebuchadnezzar invaded Jerusalem and took its leading citizens back to Babylon as captives (see 2 Kings 24 v 20b – 25 v 21). Only the poor were left behind. It was a catastrophe.

What would happen next? False prophets had been promising those exiles that they would return in a short time (Jeremiah 29 v 8). But things wouldn't be like that...

What does the LORD tell the exiles to do (v 5-6)? How did that contradict the suggestions they had been receiving from the false prophets?

How would the captives have been likely to feel about the new home?

How does God want them to relate to Babylon (v 7)? Why does he want them to do that?

Read 1 Peter 2 v 11-15

A good translation of verse 11 is "sojourners and exiles" (ESV).

In what sense is every Christian an "exile" in this world, do you think?

Where is "home" for the believer?

How does Peter tell us to pursue the welfare of our place of exile?

⊙ Apply

Some Christians will get home before others (which is a lovely way to think of death).

Are you longing for home? What difference does that make to you?

Are you praying for the place where you live now, and the people that live there? How do you seek to work for their good?

Are there ways you're in danger of being too "at home" in this world?

God's Plan for His People

Read Jeremiah 29 v 10-14

The LORD now gives the exiles some specifics: the people of Judah are going to live in exile in Babylon for 70 years. But he tells them that they can be sure that he has gracious plans to bless them.

What picture of God do we get here?

How must the people of Judah seek the LORD (v 13)?

⊙ Apply

This is a promise made to a specific group of people in a specific situation.

But how does God's promise to his people in verse 13 encourage you today?

When do you most need to remember this truth? How can it give you joy in those times?

⊙ Pray

Read Romans 8 v 28, and praise God for this truth.

~ Notes and Prayers ~

○
Day
80

Old Yoke, New Yoke

Jeremiah 30 v 1-9 (30 v 1-24)

The people of Israel and Judah were suffering under the heavy hand of foreign kings. What would salvation look like for them? Freedom from life under a king who told them what to do, presumably?!

The Days are Coming

Read Jeremiah 30 v 1-3

Earlier (in 29 v 10) the LORD had promised to bring the exiles back from Babylon after seventy years. Here, he repeats that gracious commitment. Even though they had rebelled against God and provoked his anger, the LORD promises to restore their fortunes and give back to them the land he gave to their fathers.

Throughout most of the book of Jeremiah, the words "the days are coming" (v 3) are followed with an announcement of judgment. But here we read words of grace and mercy. What amazing love the LORD shows to sinners!

⊘ Pray

God is a God of mercy. It's a simple truth, but a wonderful one—and one that should always move us to joyful praise. Spend some time thanking God for being merciful—and thank him for being merciful to you.

But First...

Read Jeremiah 30 v 4-7

God will be merciful to his people, but first they must experience great distress (v 7). "That day" will be a great day of both distress and deliverance for God's people. The Old Testament prophets often spoke of the "day of the LORD," a future day when God would execute terrible judgment against sinners.

In one sense, that day has already come in history when nations like Babylon were destroyed. But there still remains a final, decisive "day of the LORD," when all evil will be judged and dealt with.

Read Acts 17 v 31

On the day of the LORD, who will judge everyone? As Christians, how does this give us assurance as we look towards that day?

Out with the Old

Read Jeremiah 30 v 8-9

What does God promise to do (v 8)?

What will the result of this be (v 9)?

What does true freedom look like?

God's salvation isn't freedom from authority; it is freedom to submit our lives to his gracious authority. We all serve something with our lives. If we refuse to joyfully serve the LORD, we become slaves to rulers who cannot help us—and ultimately, to death.

⊘ Pray

Read Matthew 11 v 28-30. Come to the Lord Jesus now in trust-filled prayer; thank him for his authority and loving rule; ask him to help you serve him with joy today.

~ Notes and Prayers ~

His Love Goes Further Still

Jeremiah 31 v 1-14 (31 v 1-30)

After all of Judah's sin, you'd expect that God would wash his hands of them. The more we become aware of our own sin, the more we might expect God to wash his hands of us, too! But God's love is far greater than we could ever imagine.

God and His People

Read Jeremiah 31 v 1-3

The LORD promises to one day restore his intimate covenant relationship with his people (v 1). "At that time," they will once again look to him as their God, and they will be his people. Everything that had been lost will be restored!

How does God describe his own love? Why do Judah desperately need God to love like this?

Do you think that means that God doesn't care about his people's obedience at all? Why or why not?

Remember, these were people who had worshiped false gods, oppressed the poor, and even sacrificed their own children to idols! They didn't deserve God's love at all.

Read Deuteronomy 7 v 6-8

Why did God love Israel?

Why does God love you? How is this wonderful?

⊙ Apply

How does this description of God's love make you feel about coming to him when you have sinned, or neglected your duty, or when you have let yourself grow distant from him?

Shout for Joy

Read Jeremiah 31 v 4-14

Sometimes we lose sight of the fact that we cannot do anything to save ourselves. We love to think we can be our own saviors. The repetition in verses 13-14 of "I will" is a humbling, though also exciting, reminder that it is God alone who can save people, and God alone who will save people who turn to him.

Go through this passage, listing out all of the different things that the LORD says he will do for his people.

How do saved people respond to what God has done for them (v 7, 12-14)?

⊙ Apply

Is joy at being part of God's people a constant companion of yours?

I know I don't always experience this deep-down joy. If you don't either, how can we cultivate and grow a greater sense of gratitude and joy?

To make a start, choose a verse from this passage which particularly thrills you today. Pick some particular points in the next 24 hours when you're going to remember that verse.

~ Notes and Prayers ~

Day
82

The New Covenant

Jeremiah 31 v 31-34 (Jeremiah 31 v 31-40)

I f you've ever done work on your home, you'll know that sometimes it's not worth it to keep fixing the same problem again and again. There comes a point when replacing the erratic oven or unreliable hot water heater is better than repairing it every few weeks.

In the same way (though on a much more important scale!), the people of Judah couldn't keep limping along in this centuries-old pattern of disobedience and discipline, with regular temporary fixes. They needed a new covenant...

The Problem

A covenant is an agreement between two parties that governs the way they will relate to each other.

Read Jeremiah 31 v 31-34

The Lord promises to make a new covenant with his people. If you've read the Old Testament, you'll realize what a big deal that is! The covenant that the Lord made with Israel at Mount Sinai almost a millennium before was the founding document of the nation, written on stone tablets. For the Lord to make a new covenant is like the United States tearing up its beloved Constitution and writing a new, different one! But the fact is, there was a problem with the covenant that God made through Moses.

What was the problem with it (v 32)? Whose fault was this?

The Promise

How does God describe the new covenant?

How will it differ from the old one?

Under the old covenant there were a faithful few in Israel, and an unbelieving majority. But in the new covenant, there will be no such division in God's people. All of them will know him.

How is the new covenant specifically tailored to our weaknesses? How does it solve the problem that derailed the old covenant?

Read Luke 22 v 19-20

The people sitting with Christ Jesus would have known the promises of Jeremiah 31 v 31-34.

What would they have understood Jesus to be saying here? Why would they have been hugely excited?

Read 2 Corinthians 3 v 2-6, where Paul compares the old and new covenants.

How is the new covenant written on human hearts?

What is the different result of the new covenant? Why is this (Jeremiah 31 v 32 will help you here)?

⊙ Pray

Thank God the Father for his new covenant with his people. Thank the Son for bringing you into that covenant. Thank the Spirit for giving you a new heart, able to love and obey the Father.

~ Notes and Prayers ~

_____
_____
_____
_____
_____
_____
_____
_____
_____
_____
_____
_____
_____
_____
_____
_____
_____
_____
_____
_____
_____
_____
_____
_____
_____

Property Deal

Jeremiah 32 v 1-15

Buying property can be a tricky proposition. If you buy when the market is high, you risk making a bad deal. If you sell when the market is low, you risk losing money you could have made if you'd waited for a better time. But one thing is for sure: you don't want to buy land in a town that is about to be overrun by ancient Babylonian warlords. They are not known for raising property prices in areas they invade...

With Cousins like that...

Read Jeremiah 32 v 1-12

The year is 588 BC. What is the situation in Judah (v 2)?

How is King Zedekiah treating Jeremiah, and why?

Why is the offer Jeremiah's cousin makes him in verse 8 not a very good one?!

Why does Jeremiah react as he does (v 8-12)?

With a God like this...

Read Jeremiah 32 v 13-15

What was the point of this exercise? What promise was God making to a people who were about to go into exile?

Read Ezra 1 v 1-4; 2 v 1-2, 23

These events are taking place two generations later.

What is the significance of all this?

It's important to remember that the land had symbolic meaning for the people of Israel. It was more than just a real estate venture; the land was part of God's promise to his people made to Abraham over 1,000 years before (Genesis 12 v 1-3). It was where God's people could live under God's rule, enjoying his blessings. Losing their land felt to Judah as if they were losing their relationship with God!

How should Jeremiah's land deal have provided a glimmer of hope to a people who had been occupied, besieged, and were about to be exiled?

⊙ Apply

Read Hebrews 11 v 1-2, 13-16

What does it mean to be "living by faith" (v 13-16)?

How will remembering we are "foreigners and strangers" make a difference to your perspective on your day today?

How will knowing God has "prepared a city" beyond death for people of faith excite you today?

⊙ Pray

Father, thank you that you have given me a heavenly home in your perfect, eternal land. Please help me to live in light of that. Enable me not to become too attached to what I have here, which is passing away. And make where I am headed a joy and a comfort today and every day. Amen.

~ Notes and Prayers ~

Day
84

Is Anything Too Hard?

Jeremiah 32 v 16-44 (32 v 16 – 33 v 26)

We sometimes say of powerful people that it's good to have them as a friend, but bad to have them as an enemy. There are benefits to being in favor with people like that, but it's also dangerous to provoke their anger.

And if that's true of some human beings, how much more so of the LORD of all creation!

Jeremiah Speaks to God

Read Jeremiah 32 v 16-25

Jeremiah ponders the LORD's strange command to buy land in a land that is about to be destroyed (v 25). The prophet praises the LORD for his power (v 17), love (v 18), knowledge (v 19), and justice (v 18-19).

How has God shown these attributes to his people by his actions (v 20-23)?

Why do you think Jeremiah takes time to rehearse all of these glorious attributes of God? How do they help address the confusion he expresses in verse 25?

Sometimes God's ways won't make sense to us. He does things in his own way and in his own timing. When we don't understand, it's good to remember that the problem is always at our end and never at God's!

⊙ Pray

Think of a situation in your life where you do not understand the Lord's plan. Take time to praise him for his wisdom, power and love. Commit yourself to trusting him no matter what happens!

God Speaks to Jeremiah

Read Jeremiah 32 v 26-35

What does God remind Jeremiah of (v 26-27)?

How is this an answer to Jeremiah's confusion? What does it teach us about being a follower of God?

The Lord responds to the prophet by affirming his praise. Everything Jeremiah said about God is true and important for understanding the Lord's dealings with Jerusalem. With God, there is no impossible: either in bringing justice, or giving mercy.

Whose idea was the Babylonian invasion (v 28)?

What had the people of Judah done to deserve their punishment (v 29-35)?

Read Jeremiah 32 v 36-44

What promises does God make? Given what's happening (v 24), why would these promises have been hard to truly trust in?

So why is remembering verse 27 crucial?

It is amazing that we can be called friends of the all-powerful, living God (James 2 v 23; John 15 v 15). But we mustn't forget that a powerful, holy God is a terrible enemy to have (Hebrews 10 v 31).

⊙ Pray

It's only as we realize that God is a holy God, who will bring judgment, that we can appreciate his promises to bless us, and his power to do so. Thank him now for who he is and what he does for you.

~ Notes and Prayers ~

Day
85

Remember the Rekabites

Jeremiah 35 v 1-19 (34 v 1 – 35 v 19)

The book of Jeremiah reads like a chronicle of the sins of God's people: immorality, violence, greed, and idolatry. But now we have an example of an honorable (though, admittedly, weird!) group of people who had recently arrived in Jerusalem.

A Faithful Family

Read Jeremiah 35 v 1-11

The Rekabites were a small family with an impressive pedigree. Their father, Jehonadab, appears in 2 Kings 10 as a faithful man who fought on the side of the LORD against idol-worshipers.

What instructions did Jehonadab leave his family about how to live (Jeremiah 35 v 6-10)?

What was the cost of obeying their forefather, do you think?

We don't know why Jehonadab insisted on this way of life. Nothing in Scripture speaks against drinking wine or settling down and building homes.

Why were the Rekabites now living in Jerusalem (v 11)?

Why do you think the LORD instructs Jeremiah to offer wine to the Rekabites (v 2)? What is he trying to prove?

They Should be a Lesson to you

Read Jeremiah 35 v 12-19

This is a strange little story. But the LORD has a point to make.

What is it (v 13-14, 16)? What should Judah have been doing?

What would happen to them now (v 17)?

Look at God's promise to the Rekabites (v 18-19). How is this a lesson to Judah of what they could have enjoyed, had they obeyed their "father," the LORD?

⊙ Apply

This passage asks the question, if the Rekabites obeyed their dad in relatively minor things, why did the people of Judah have no desire to obey the moral commands given by the God of the universe?

Think about your own life. Whose will and desires influence your behavior most?

- *Your spouse's?*

- *Your boss'?*

- *Your friends'?*

- *The fashion magazines'?*

- *A TV program's?*

- *Or the LORD's?*

When, and why, do you find yourself more motivated to please others than to please God?

How will you please God today? Is there any way you need to turn disobedience into obedience to your Father?

⊙ Pray

Speak to God about you answers to the "Apply" section above:

Our Father in heaven, your will be done...

~ Notes and Prayers ~

Day
86

Burning
the Bible

Jeremiah 36 v 1-4, 20-32 (36 v 1 – 38 v 28)

Imagine you are sick. Looking for relief from your illness, you visit a doctor who gives you a prescription for medicine. After visiting the pharmacy you come home and put the bottle of pills on your kitchen counter, where they remain unopened and untouched.

Several days later, you call the doctor back and complain that you're still sick. What do you think he would tell you?!

The Prescription

Read Jeremiah 36 v 1-4

The year is 605 BC (we've rewound slightly to before Babylon invaded). The people of Jerusalem are relatively independent, but the Babylonian Empire is gobbling up small nations all around the area. The LORD tells Jeremiah to write out all of his sermons and prophecies onto a scroll (v 2).

Why (v 3)?

If Judah listen to this prescription, what will God do?

The King's Response

After reading the contents of the scroll in the temple, Baruch—Jeremiah's scribe—is ushered into the presence of the king to read the LORD's warning.

Read Jeremiah 36 v 20-25

What did the king do (v 23)? What is the significance of this action?

Why do you think he did it?

Read Psalm 19 v 7-14

How does David's attitude to God's word compare to his descendant Jehoiakim's?

How do you see these two attitudes in the world you live in?

Do you ever see them struggling against each other in your heart?

The Unstoppable Word of God

Read Jeremiah 36 v 26-32

The king destroyed the scroll; Jeremiah rewrites it (v 32). And the existence of the book of Jeremiah in our Bibles shows that Jehoiakim's plan didn't work! The word of God is living and active, sharper than a sword (Hebrews 4 v 12). Rebellious humanity can hate the word of the LORD, even burn the word of the LORD. But it can never suppress or defeat God's unstoppable truth!

⊙ Apply

God's word is like a prescription for medicine: it only helps if you follow the instructions and apply it!

Do you cultivate a soft, teachable heart towards God's word? Are there bad attitudes which harden your heart toward his words?

Is there any way you know what God says, but are ignoring him? Read James 1 v 22.

~ Notes and Prayers ~

$$\left(\begin{array}{c}\text{Day}\\ 87\end{array}\right)$$

The End,
at Last

Jeremiah 39 v 1-14 (39 v 1 – 43 v 13)

Sometimes in a tragic movie, the anticipation of disaster is more tense than when it arrives. There is almost a sense of relief when the aliens finally take over, the crime is committed, or the heart is broken.

After 38 chapters of warning in the book of Jeremiah, we've finally reached the point where the city of Jerusalem falls. And after 40 years of being mocked, imprisoned, and publicly denounced, the prophet Jeremiah is finally vindicated.

Read Jeremiah 39 v 1-14

A Terrible Vindication

The account of the destruction of the city is relatively brief. And it seems that the details that are included in the account were specifically chosen to show that God's prophetic word had come true.

Look at the events in our passage and see how they fulfill the earlier word of the LORD.

Event		Prophecy	
	Jeremiah 39 v 3		Jeremiah 1 v 15
	Jeremiah 39 v 5		Jeremiah 32 v 4
	Jeremiah 39 v 8		Jeremiah 21 v 10
	Jeremiah 39 v 11-14		Jeremiah 1 v 17-19
	Jeremiah 39 v 1-10		Jeremiah 1 v 11-12

A Crucial Lesson

If we learn nothing else from the book of Jeremiah, we must learn that God always tells the truth. God never lies about what he will do, and he always has the power to do what he says (see 1 v 12).

Human beings aren't reliable in the same way. We occasionally deceive or manipulate others with our words. Sometimes we speak honestly about our plans, but then don't have the power to bring them to pass. Illness, a freak snowstorm, or a charging troop of capuchin monkeys can stop us doing what we've planned to do. But God never has that problem. He always does what he says he will do.

The destruction of Jerusalem was brutal. The city was burned, the princes were slaughtered, and the king was blinded, fettered and led into captivity.

How do you think the captives felt about the LORD? About Jeremiah? About their own sin?

How do you think the people who were left behind felt (39 v 10)?

⊘ Apply

God does what he says he will do. How will that truth affect how you:

• *think about his warnings (e.g. 1 Corinthians 6 v 9-10)?*

• *think about his promises (e.g. Matthew 16 v 18)?*

⊘ Pray

Praise God that his word is truthful, and that he is able to keep his word. Ask him to help you trust his word today. Tell him about any situations in which you find it hard to remember that he is watching to ensure his word comes true.

~ Notes and Prayers ~

Day
88

The Destroyer Destroyed

Jeremiah 50 v 1-16 (44 v 1 – 50 v 46)

Throughout the book of Jeremiah, the armies of Babylon have loomed menacingly in the distance, pictured as an unstoppable force ready to be unleashed. Now that they've finally destroyed Jerusalem and taken its people captive, what will Babylon do next?

The Worm has Turned

Read Jeremiah 50 v 1-3

What will happen to Babylon (v 3)?

What effect will this have on the respect that people have for Bel and Marduk (false Babylonian gods—v 2)?

Most nations in Jeremiah's day believed that each nation had its own gods, and those gods protected that nation and blessed it, based on its faithfulness and obedience. When one nation defeated another, it was sometimes assumed that the victorious nation's deity was stronger than the defeated one. So the LORD's message here is clear: he is greater than Babylon and all of its gods.

The Reason

Read Jeremiah 50 v 4-16

The Babylonians thought that they would not be held accountable for their actions against Jerusalem because the people of Judah had rebelled against the LORD (v 7). But he condemns them for their actions anyway.

Read through the passage and identify the places where the LORD speaks against:

- *Their idolatry and sin against him.*
- *The Babylonians hurting his people and destroying his city.*
- *The joy they took in destroying Jerusalem.*
- *The violence (plundering) of the Babylonian army.*

⊙ Apply

It's significant that the LORD holds Babylon accountable for their sin against him. God is the God of every person in every nation; he will judge everyone for their sins against him.

Read Romans 1 v 18-25

Why is it right and fair that everyone on earth faces judgment for their rejection of God (v 19-21)?

How does that impact your thinking and prayers about your friends who don't know Christ? And about foreign missions?

⊙ Pray

Lord, thank you that you work out your purposes even through people who reject you. You deserve the worship of every person on earth. You are just in all of your ways. Please help me to honor you in the way that I should. Please show me how I can use my prayers, my words and my finances to further the spread of your saving gospel to all nations. Amen.

~ Notes and Prayers ~

Day
89

The Story Ends... or Does it?

Jeremiah 52 v 1-23, 31-34 (51 v 1 – 52 v 34)

The book of Jeremiah doesn't deliver a lot of sunny moments. Between the prophecies of destruction and the actual accounts of the destruction, there is not too much to be hopeful about. How will this kind of book end?

The City

Read Jeremiah 52 v 1-11

These verses are almost exactly identical to 2 Kings 24 v 18 – 25 v 7. And we've already encountered the content of Jeremiah 52 v 4-11 in 39 v 1-7. We're supposed to see this as the end result of all of Jeremiah's work. Very few people listened and there was little repentance. So Jerusalem was destroyed. Perhaps this needs repeating so that *we* listen.

The Temple

Read Jeremiah 52 v 12-23

What happened to the temple?

The temple was Judah's heart: the place God lived among his people, where his people could make sacrifice for their sins to stay in relationship with him.

How are these verses a total catastrophe?

Like Adam and Eve being driven out of the Garden of Eden (Genesis 3 v 21-24), the people of Judah were paying a steep price for their sin.

The King

Read Jeremiah 52 v 31-34

On the face of it, this seems like a very strange ending for the book of Jeremiah. Jehoiachin was released from prison and allowed to live in Babylon. So what? Why does this matter?

In fact, this is hugely significant—because God had promised King David that his son would always sit on the throne of Jerusalem (2 Samuel 7 v 11-14).

So how are these verses a glimmer of hope?

The message of Jeremiah is that Jerusalem's destruction and exile will not prevent God from bringing about his plan to save his people by sending his Son to be their King. God's love for his people is unshakable.

Read Matthew 1 v 1-17

Whose family tree is this (v 1)?

How do the events described in Jeremiah 52 form part of it (Matthew 1 v 11)?

What was God doing, even in the darkest days of Old Testament Judah?

⊙ Apply

How does the end of Jeremiah give you hope and confidence as you consider your own sins and adverse circumstances? How about when you are confronted by the wider failings of God's people?

How has the book of Jeremiah given you:

• *a greater view of God?*

• *a greater appreciation for Christ?*

⊙ Pray

Lord, I praise you for your faithfulness to your people. Thank you for loving us enough to discipline us, and thank you for never abandoning us because of our sin. Thank you that you brought your Son, my King, into the world at just the right time. Thank you that through him I can know forgiveness and enjoy the presence of your Spirit. Amen.

~ Notes and Prayers ~

Day
90

Ninetieth-Day Reflection

Ruth; 1 Corinthians; Jeremiah

As you come to the end of these ninety days of devotionals, it is a good time to reflect on how the Lord has been speaking to you in these particular portions of his word, how he has been exciting you about his Son, and how he has been changing you by his Spirit. After all, God's word is not meant simply to inform us, but to transform us.

The Book of Ruth

If you had to sum up the message of Ruth in one or two sentences, how would you do it?

_____

_____

_____

_____

What one truth about God that you saw in Ruth has most remained with you since?

_____

_____

_____

Looking back, in what ways did the Spirit use the book of Ruth to cause you to lean on God more heavily and joyfully?

_____

_____

_____

_____

The Book of 1 Corinthians

If you had to sum up the message of 1 Corinthians in one or two sentences, how would you do it?

_____

_____

_____

_____

What one truth about God that you saw in 1 Corinthians has most remained with you since?

_____

_____

_____

Looking back, in what ways did the Spirit use the book of 1 Corinthians to change your thinking about, and behavior within, your church?

_____

_____

_____

The Book of Jeremiah

If you had to sum up the message of Jeremiah in one or two sentences, how would you do it?

_____

_____

_____

_____

What one truth about God that you saw in Jeremiah has most remained with you since?

_____

_____

_____

In what ways has the Spirit used the book of Jeremiah to provoke you to take God's judgment more seriously and appreciate his salvation more gratefully?

_____

_____

_____

_____

⊙ Pray

Father, I thank you for your word. Thank you for its variety. Thank you for its depth. Thank you that each part of it points me to the glories of your Son, my Lord Jesus Christ. Father, please would your word dwell in me richly. Please would I recall the truths and challenges of these three parts of your word to mind, at the moments when I need to be excited, challenged or comforted by them. Please would you show me who I can encourage around me with the truths you have revealed to me. Amen.

EXPLORE

BY THE BOOK

More from the series...

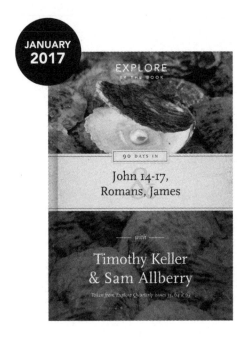

Timothy Keller and Sam Allberry take you through three key New Testament sections. Experience the joy of the gospel in Romans, a book that has changed history so many times. Wrestle with the challenging applications of James' letter to the church. And listen to the Lord's teaching the night before he died, as recounted by John.

" Reliable, faithful and accessible. Fantastic for anyone who wants to spend regular time in God's word. "

Steve Timmis, Global Director, Acts 29

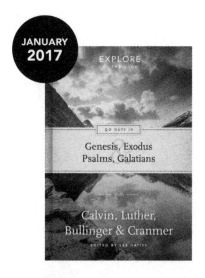

JANUARY 2017

Let four of the great Bible teachers of the Reformation—John Calvin, Martin Luther, Heinrich Bullinger and Thomas Cranmer—teach you the Scriptures, day by day. Edited by Lee Gatiss, this devotional brings the work of these sixteenth-century giants to life in an engaging and accessible way.

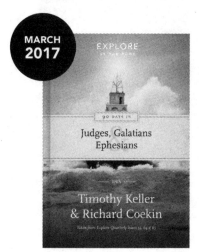

MARCH 2017

Join Timothy Keller, Senior Pastor of Redeemer Presbyterian Church, Manhattan, and Richard Coekin, Director of the Co-Mission church-planting network in London, UK. They will take you through the gripping days of the judges, the gospel freedom of Galatians, and the Christ-centered glories of Ephesians.

the**good**book
COMPANY

www.thegoodbook.com/explorebythebook

EXPLORE
DAILY DEVOTIONAL

Meet the rest of the Explore family. *Explore Quarterly* is a numbered, dated resource that works through the entire Bible every seven years in quarterly publications and features contributions from trusted Bible teachers such as Sam Allberry, Al Mohler, and HB Charles Jr. The *Explore App* brings open-Bible devotionals to your smartphone or tablet, enabling you to choose between dated studies, studies on a specific book, and topical sets.

www.thegoodbook.com/explore

thegoodbook
COMPANY

Opening up the Bible

At The Good Book Company, we are dedicated to helping Christians and local churches grow. We believe that God's growth process always starts with hearing clearly what he has said to us through his timeless word—the Bible.

Ever since we opened our doors in 1991, we have been striving to produce resources that honor God in the way the Bible is used. We have grown to become an international provider of user-friendly resources to the Christian community, with believers of all backgrounds and denominations using our Bible studies, books, evangelistic resources, DVD-based courses and training events.

We want to equip ordinary Christians to live for Christ day by day, and churches to grow in their knowledge of God, their love for one another, and the effectiveness of their outreach.

Call us for a discussion of your needs or visit one of our local websites for more information on the resources and services we provide.

Your friends at The Good Book Company

NORTH AMERICA		thegoodbook.com		866 244 2165
UK & EUROPE		thegoodbook.co.uk		0333 123 0880
AUSTRALIA		thegoodbook.com.au		(02) 6100 4211
NEW ZEALAND		thegoodbook.co.nz		(+64) 3 343 2463

 WWW.CHRISTIANITYEXPLORED.ORG
Our partner site is a great place for those exploring the Christian faith, with a clear explanation of the good news, powerful testimonies and answers to difficult questions.